3·90

# FROM LAIRDS T(

# FROM LAIRDS
# TO LOUNS

## COUNTRY AND BURGH LIFE
## IN ABERDEEN
## 1600–1800

*edited by*
DAVID STEVENSON

ABERDEEN UNIVERSITY PRESS

First published 1986
Aberdeen University Press
A member of the Pergamon Group

© Centre for Scottish Studies, University of Aberdeen 1986

**British Library Cataloguing in Publication Data**

From lairds to louns: country and burgh
  life in Aberdeen 1600–1800
  1. Aberdeen (Grampian)—History
  I. Stevenson, David, *1942-*
  941.2′3506     DA890.A2

ISBN 0-08-034514-X

PRINTED IN GREAT BRITAIN
THE UNIVERSITY PRESS
ABERDEEN

# CONTENTS

# ILLUSTRATIONS

# PREFACE

This is the third work to appear in the occasional series sponsored by the Centre for Scottish Studies, University of Aberdeen, and published by Aberdeen University Press. The first of the series, *New light on medieval Aberdeen* (1985), sought to present to a wider public the results of recent research on the early history of the burgh. This volume is similar in intention but deals with a rather later period and includes the results of recent investigations into the shire as well as the burgh. The volume is based on the papers given at a day conferences entitled *Lairds, landscape and life* held in Aberdeen on 2 November, 1985, and thanks are due to Rod Gunson of the Department of Geography, the Centre's Conference Organiser, and to the Department of Adult Education and Extra-Mural Studies which helped organise that event. I am also most grateful to the authors of the papers, whose enthusiasm and clarity in describing their research made the conference both entertaining and stimulating, to Dr Roy Bridges who chaired the conference, and to the audience of nearly two hundred, whose numbers testified to the growing interest in local history in the North East.

There are two main differences between the conference programme and the contents of this volume. Dr Coull's conference paper has been summarised, as a full version of it has already been published; and an extra paper by Gordon DesBrisay, originally read at a Scottish Records Association conference, has been added as it fits in very well with the other papers.

Illustrations 1 and 2, taken from H. Hamilton (ed.), *An Aberdeenshire estate* (1946) are reproduced by permission of the Friends of Aberdeen University Library, as the volume is a publication of the Third Spalding Club. Illustrations 3 and 4 appear by permission of the Town Clerk of Aberdeen. Illustration 5 is taken from the painting by G.G. Burr published in his *Old landmarks of Aberdeen* (1896), and 6 is from *Charters and other writs illustrating the history of the royal burgh of Aberdeen* (1890).

DAVID STEVENSON
Director of the Centre for Scottish Studies
and Reader in Scottish History,
University of Aberdeen

# THE PATTERN OF LAND OWNERSHIP IN ABERDEENSHIRE IN THE SEVENTEENTH AND EIGHTEENTH CENTURIES

## ROBIN CALLANDER

There is little detailed information available about the pattern of landownership in Aberdeenshire before the seventeenth century. However, it is clear that the number of landowners was increasing and the size of the larger estates decreasing during the proceeding five centuries. The speculative line in Figure 1 indicates this general trend, and many examples could be cited to illustrate it. For example, the lands of Mar which reverted to the Crown in 1435 were shared between 150 proprietors by the late sixteenth century. The proliferation of cadet branches also demonstrates this trend with, for example, the four legitimate sons of the fourteenth century Sir John Forbes (Black Lip) giving rise to four dozen landowning branches during the next two hundred years.

This longstanding trend was reversed at some point during the seventeenth century, and throughout the eighteenth century the number of landowners in Aberdeenshire continued to decline and the proportion of the county held by the larger estates to grow. Valuation rolls provide a detailed means of examining these changes in the pattern of landownership from the mid seventeenth century onwards. The valuation rolls were based on a system of 'valued rent', which had first been introduced in 1643 for taxation purposes and continued to be used into the nineteenth century. The 'valued rent' was the real value of each property as valued in 1656. This fixed value became increasingly divorced from real money as time passed, but it continued to be the basis of assessment, and provides a consistent valuation for comparisons throughout the period. No measurements of the acreage of estates is available for the seventeenth and eighteenth centuries and it should be noted that the valued rent figures underestimate the area of the county held by the larger estates.

The valuation rolls were compiled by parish and the landowners in that parish, here referred to as the 'parish heritors', were listed with the valued rent of the land they owned there. However, because there were always some landowners who had land in more than one parish, the total number of 'parish heritors' in the county (calculated by adding together the numbers of heritors in each parish) was always more than the actual number of landowners in Aberdeenshire. In this paper, therefore, a distinction is drawn between the two terms and the use of 'parish heritors' is restricted to figures deriving directly from the parish by parish lists in the valuation rolls.

TABLE 1

*The Number of Heritors in Aberdeenshire, 1667, 1796, 1771 and 1791*

| | No. of parishes | 1667 Total no. of heritors | Av/ parish | 1696 Total no. of heritors | Av/ parish | 1771 Total no. of heritors | Av/ parish | 1791 Total no. of heritors | Av/ parish |
|---|---|---|---|---|---|---|---|---|---|
| Deeside & Alford | 23 | 246 | 10.7 | 197 | 9.4 | 178 | 5.6 | 116 | 5.0 |
| Huntly & Garioch | 22 | 194 | 8.8 | 128 | 5.8 | 107 | 4.9 | 88 | 4.0 |
| Turriff, Ellon & Deer | 26 | 259 | 10.0 | 182 | 7.0 | 137 | 5.3 | 153 | 5.9 |
| Aberdeen | 11 | 100 | 8.8 | 67 | 6.1 | 76 | 6.9 | 90 | 8.2 |
| Total | 82 | 799 | 9.7 | 574 | 7.0 | 448 | 5.5 | 447 | 5.5 |

1667 is the first year for which a comprehensive valuation roll is available. There were then 799 parish heritors in Aberdeenshire but, due to the landowners with land in more than one parish, there were only 621 landowners. The pattern of parish heritors, an average of 9.7 per parish, was fairly consistent throughout the county (Table 1). However, the distribution of land, in terms of valued rent, between the 621 landowners was very uneven. It was a pattern of relatively few large landowners and many small ones. For example, 8.1% of the landowners (the largest 51) held 44% of the county between them, while 81% (the smallest 503) held 35.3% (Table 2). A further feature of this pattern was the importance of a small number of long established landowning families. Twenty out of the twenty-five largest landowners shared seven family names: Gordon, Forbes, Fraser, Erskine, Keith, Hay and Irvine, and these families had in all over a hundred landowning branches amongst Aberdeenshire's 621 landowners. Other important landowning families included the Burnetts, Farquharsons, Leslies and Leiths, which had about fifty landowning branches between them. In total,

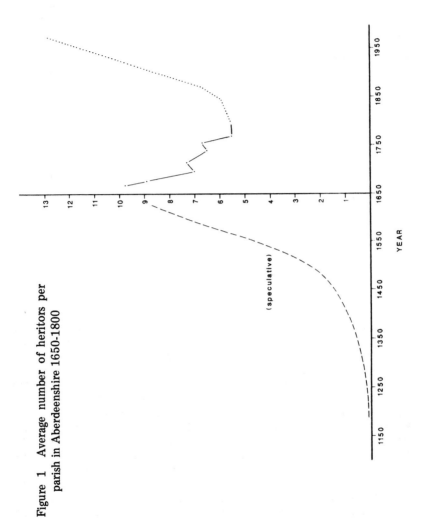

Figure 1 Average number of heritors per parish in Aberdeenshire 1650-1800

around twenty-five family groups involved nearly a third of the landowners in Aberdeenshire, and between them they held over two-thirds of the county's valued rent.

These main families had dominated landownership in Aberdeenshire since the fourteenth century, and they were interrelated through marriage and a web of kinship ties. The connections tended to be closest amongst the largest landowners, as illustrated by Mary Erskine, the only woman in the list of Aberdeenshire's twenty-five largest landlowners in 1667. She was herself sixth in the rating, sister to the earl of Mar (eleventh) mother of the Earl Marischal (second) and also stepmother to the 2nd earl of Panmure (fifth). The 2nd earl had only inherited his title in 1661, and the 1st earl had been married to Mary Erskine for 25 years, though she was his third wife and he had been her second husband.

The decline in the number of landowners in Aberdeenshire was already underway in the years immediately after 1667, suggesting that the maximum number from the increases of earlier centuries had been passed in the early to mid seventeenth century. The average number of parish heritors in the county dropped from 9.7 in 1667 to 8.9 in 1674 and was down to 7.0 by 1696. This overall decline occurred in every district of the county and reduced the total number of parish heritors by a quarter. The fall in the total number of landowners in the county was even steeper, because the increased concentration of ownership resulted in an increasing proportion of landowners holding land in more than one parish.

The trend towards a reconcentration of landownership in Aberdeenshire continued during the eighteenth century, although not in a consistent manner. Between 1696 and 1715, the average number of heritors per parish actually increased slightly from 7.0 to 7.3, before declining to 6.5 by 1741. By 1754 the number had gone up again to 6.7, before falling sharply to 5.5 by 1771. Thus between 1667 and 1771 the total number of parish heritors in the county fell from 799 to 448, with a correspondingly greater reduction in the number of landowners from 621 to 250. The concentrated pattern of landownership by 1771 resulting in nearly a third (seventy-four) of all the county's landowners holding land in more than one parish. The greatest of these was the earl of Aberdeen who had land in eighteen parishes. He also had major estates in other counties, as did Aberdeenshire's other larger landowners.

The decline in the number of landowners to just 250 by 1771 resulted almost entirely from the disappearance of the

TABLE 2

*The Structure of Landownership in Aberdeenshire, 1667 and 1771*

| Valued rent £s Scots | 1667 | | | 1771 | | |
|---|---|---|---|---|---|---|
| | No. of owners | % of owners | % total valued rent | No. of owners | % of owners | % total valued rent |
| Over £2,000 | 21 | 3.3 | 27.5 | 27 | 10.8 | 49.6 |
| £500 — £2,000 | 97 | 15.6 | 35.5 | 83 | 33.2 | 32.9 |
| Under £500 | 503 | 81.1 | 35.3 | 140 | 56.0 | 12.3 |
| Kirks, institutions, corporations | | | 1.8 | | | 5.2 |
| Total | 621 | 100 | 100 | 250 | 100 | 100 |

smaller estates (Figure 2 and Table 2). The number of land-owners with lands valued at less than £500 declined by 363, and their share of the county fell by nearly two thirds. The number of landowners with lands above this size stayed remarkably constant (119 and 114), with the most significant change being the increase in the share of the largest owners to 50% of the shire's value (Table 2). Thus, even with this reduced number of land-owners the basic pattern of a few large landowners and many more small landowners still continued. In 1771, for example, while 27 individuals held 50% of the value, 90% was held by 133 out of the 250 landowners, and only 10% by the remaining 117.

Although the share of the county owned by landowners with lands worth over £2000 nearly doubled between 1667 and 1771, there were important changes in other ranks. Seventeen of the top twenty-five owners in 1667 had suffered the complete loss or substantial reduction of their estates by 1771 due to either military or financial failure. For example, as a consequence of the Jacobite risings, the earl of Dunfermline's lands were forfeited in 1690, and in 1715 the estates of the earls of Mar, Marischal and Panmure met the same fate. The earls of Errol, Irvines of Drum and three top Forbes landowners all suffered reductions in their estates due to financial decline and misadventure. However, families like these remained major landowners even after they had dropped out of the top twenty-five. The changes that occurred between 1667 and 1771 were little more than an interchange between top and middling land-owners, with old landowning families moving up through the

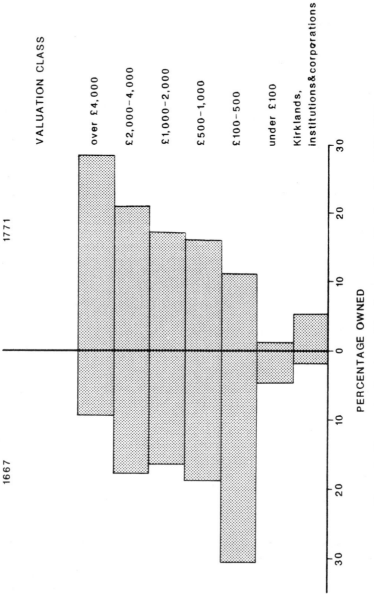

Figure 2  Changes in structure of landownership, Aberdeenshire 1667, 1771

ranks to overtake those in decline. Thus Gordon landowners obtained a clear dominance of the county, owning around 30% of its value between them. Another 40% was owned by eleven of Aberdeenshire's other traditional landowning families. These were, in order of holding, Forbes, Duffs, Farquharsons, Keiths, Hays, Leiths, Frasers, Grants, Irvines, Burnetts and Leslies.

The dramatic drop in the number of landowners between 1667 and 1771 was, however, only a net decrease. Throughout the period, newcomers had been buying into the landed classes because of the advantages that the ownership of land conferred. In the seventeenth century these new landowners were principally wealthy merchants or successful lawyers, soldiers or administrators. In the first half of the eighteenth century they included many Scots who had made their money abroad, typically as soldiers of fortune or as merchants in Europe or new spheres like the East Indies. By the second half of the eighteenth century, when Scotland's economy was becoming increasingly active and diverse, more of the new landowners had obtained their wealth within Scotland.

The demand for land from these newcomers and the younger sons of existing landed families had produced an overall increase in parish heritors in the area around the burgh of Aberdeen by 1771 and in the east of the county in general by 1791 (Figure 3 and Table 1). However, it was not until during the first half of the nineteenth century that this trend was sufficient to increase the number of parish heritors in the county as a whole. During the last quarter of the eighteenth century, the number of landowners continued to fall, and was down to 236 by 1800.

The newcomers had little influence on the pattern of estates during the seventeenth and eighteenth centuries, usually only acquiring small estates. In 1771-1800 the largest owners continued to increase their share of the county with only minor adjustments in their own ranks. By the end of the century, 70% of Aberdeenshire's valued rent was held by just sixty-three individuals and, despite increases in the numbers of landowners during the nineteenth century, it was not until the present century that there was any significant change in that estate structure.

In the changing social circumstances of the seventeenth and eighteenth centuries, the larger traditional landowning families maintained their political, economic and social dominance of Aberdeenshire by strengthening their hold on the land. This pattern seen for Aberdeenshire, of a century and half of reconcentration, was also a national pattern. Loretta Timperley has estimated that Scotland had 9500 landowners in 1700, 8500

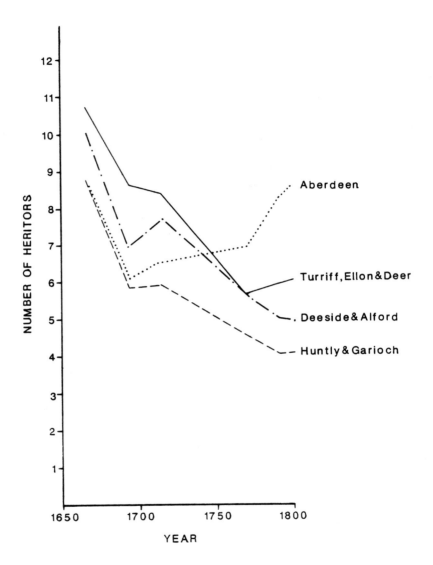

Figure 3    Average number of heritors per parish, by district within
Aberdeenshire, 1667-1800

in the mid eighteenth century and 8000 at the beginning of the nineteenth century.

The reasons for this marked change in the pattern of land-ownership from the mid seventeenth century, and the consequences of the replacement of small landowners by the large estates of the great landowners, are important topics that bear on many aspects of Scottish history and deserve further research.

REFERENCES

Grant, I., Landlords and land management in Northeast Scotland, 1750-1850 (Ph.D. thesis, University of Edinburgh, 1979).

Stuart, J. (ed.), *List of pollable persons within the shire of Aberdeen, 1696* (2 vols., Aberdeen, 1844).

Tayler, A. & H. (eds.), *The valuation of the county of Aberdeen for the year 1667* (Third Spalding Club, 1933).

Tayler, A. & H. (eds.), *The Jacobite cess roll for the county of Aberdeen in 1715* (Third Spalding Club, 1932).

Timperley, L.R., Landownership in Scotland in the eighteenth century (Ph.D. thesis, University of Edinburgh, 1977).

Timperley, L.R. (ed.), *A directory of landownership in Scotland, c. 1770*, (Scottish Record Society, 1976).

# AGRICULTURE IN ABERDEENSHIRE IN THE SEVENTEENTH AND EARLY EIGHTEENTH CENTURIES: CONTINUITY AND CHANGE

## IAN WHYTE

The traditional interpretation of the development of agriculture in Scotland has involved the idea of an Agricultural Revolution during the later eighteenth and early nineteenth centuries. This Revolution changed the face of the countryside and the character of rural society within the space of a couple of generations. In the North East it produced the highly commercialised rural landscape of large farms and peripheral crofts and the rural society of the ploughman and the bothy which continued up to and beyond the First World War. Pre-improvement agriculture was dismissed as uniformly inefficient and primitive, having scarcely advanced in techniques and productivity since medieval times.[1] One reason for this interpretation was an undue reliance on descriptions of pre-improvement agriculture by eighteenth-century writers who included Archibald Grant of Monymusk, one of the first 'Improvers' in Aberdeenshire. The problem was that these men were propagandists with a vested interest in drawing unfavourable contrasts between contemporary farming practices and the new systems which they were trying to disseminate.

Such views have been modified by recent detailed studies of seventeenth-century estate documents. While this work has not identified a hitherto hidden 'Agricultural Revolution' in Scotland during the seventeenth century comparable to the one which has been claimed for England,[2] it has shown that many aspects of agricultural change which had traditionally been ascribed to the eighteenth century began a century earlier.[3] Seventeenth-century Scottish agriculture had not been stagnant; there had been changes in farming practices and in the organisation of farming society which paved the way for the more impressive and more widely-advertised changes of the era of Improvement. Such developments, nevertheless, took place against a background of underlying continuity in the basic character of farming and rural life.

This article pursues these complementary themes of continuity and change with regard to agriculture in Aberdeenshire during the seventeenth and early eighteenth centuries. One aim is to identify some of the distinctive features of the shire's farming systems during this period and how they varied from one region to another. In trying to pinpoint some of the ways in which farming changed during this century and some of the implications which these changes had for the future, it is necessary to consider influences such as rural social structure and farm and holding sizes, and to understand the nature of the relationship between landlord and tenant. It is important to stress, however, that our understanding of agriculture and rural society in Aberdeenshire during this period is still very imperfect. There is considerable scope for further research and some of the themes on which our knowledge is weakest, together with the sources which may be capable of providing the answers, will be indicated.

**Regional variations in farming within Aberdeenshire**

Aberdeenshire is a very varied county in its topography and environmental conditions. This is reflected in marked contrasts in present-day farming within the county and it is likely that marked regional and local differences in farming patterns also existed in the past. It is no easy matter to pick out these variations from the sources. Estate papers, being concerned primarily with tenancy, rents and arrears, only shed light on this theme indirectly. The rents which farmers paid nevertheless provide some clues to geographical contrasts in agriculture. Farmers in more arable-oriented areas paid much of their rent in grain. Those in districts in which there was a balance between crop and livestock production paid rents in both grain and money, while those in the pastoral uplands frequently paid rent in money only. This allows us to divide the county into three general types of region (Figure 1, bottom right). At a more detailed scale contemporary topographic descriptions provide indications of variations in the rural economy at a parish level. Figure 1 shows this for one group of parishes based on statements made by one early eighteenth century writer.[4] This is still a crude way of distinguishing different types of farming. There were doubtless important variations at a local scale too but nobody has yet tried to identify them. This could be done in many parts of Scotland by using the inventories of farmers' possessions, including crops and livestock, contained in the testaments which were lodged with local commissary courts. Detailed analysis of these provides a wealth of data on the rural economy in the seventeenth and eighteenth centuries but unfortunately

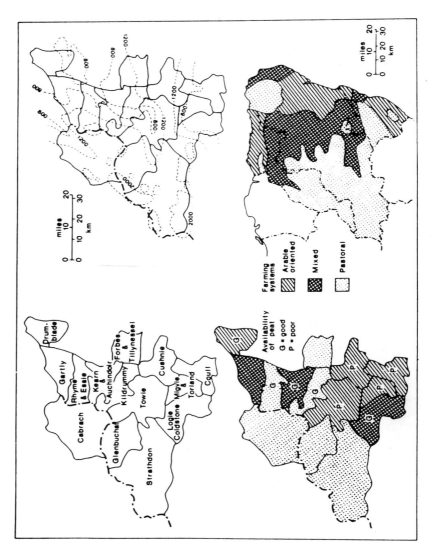

Figure 1   Farming regions in a group of Aberdeenshire parishes
and in the shire as a whole, 17th and early 18th century

all the Registers of Testaments for the Aberdeen commissariot prior to 1715 were destroyed by fire.[5]

A general point about farming is that during the seventeenth and early eighteenth centuries crops were grown virtually everywhere in the county, even in remote upland glens. In such areas the amount of arable land was often very small, and the returns to the husbandman meagre, but at a time when cereals were a major element in most people's diet it was vital to try and produce enough to meet the needs of the local population rather than rely on importing surplus grain from the lowlands — a source of supply which could dry up after a poor harvest. On the other hand even the areas which concentrated on cereal production always maintained a good deal of land in rough pasture  for grazing. Given that animal manure was essential for maintaining soil fertility, and that fodder crops like turnips and sown grasses were not grown, much potentially cultivable land had to be maintained in pasture. If we were able to go back and look at the Aberdeenshire landscape in the seventeenth century our first reaction might be surprise at how much land was being kept out of cultivation as rough pasture, outfield in fallow, peat moss, and undrained bottom land. Infield-outfield farming was geared to an essentially pastoral economy.

### Infield-outfield farming and crop rotations

The perception of arable farming in Aberdeenshire and more generally throughout Scotland during the pre-improvement period has been strongly influenced, directly or at second hand, by James Anderson who produced the county report on farming in Aberdeenshire for the Board of Agriculture in 1794,[6] and by James Wilson who in 1902 wrote an article on old farming practices in the county.[7] Wilson drew up a diagrammatic summary of a typical Scottish field system which, explicitly or otherwise, has formed the basis of most historians' descriptions ever since. Wilson divided the arable land into two categories, infield and outfield. The former, on the best land, received most of the animal manure and other fertilizers and usually took up about a third of the arable area. It was cropped continuously with an unending rotation of a year of bere, a hardy form of barley, followed by two years of oats. Most of the outfield was under rough pasture at any time. It was divided into folds and faughs. The folds made up about a third of the outfield. Portions of it were manured by feeding livestock on it during the summer, then ploughed, and cropped with oats (without any further manure) until returns had fallen to such a low level that

further cultivation was abandoned and the land was left to recover for a few years. The faughs consisted of outfield which
was periodically ploughed up and cropped for two or three
years without any manure. Reading Wilson's account it is clear
that he was deliberately generalising and that there must have
been considerable variation in cropping patterns within Scotland and, at a smaller scale, Aberdeenshire.

The kind of variations which are likely to have occurred include differences in the ratio of cultivated land to rough pasture,
contrasts in the proportion of infield to outfield, and differences in farming practices such as crops, rotations and fertilizers.
There are indications, naturally enough, that the amount of
land in cultivation was greater in lowland districts, and that the
proportion of infield was higher on the more fertile soils. Details of rotations and crop yields at this period are difficult to
obtain; they may be mentioned in farm leases, and can sometimes be reconstructed from estate accounts which include information on the cultivation of the mains ('home farm') when it
was under the direct management of the proprietor.

Estate papers and other sources show that in some respects
cultivation practices in Aberdeenshire during the later seventeenth century were behind those in more advanced areas like
the Lothians. For one thing, relatively little wheat was grown in
the county. Wheat was the highest-priced cereal but was more
demanding in its requirements than the hardier bere and oats. It
is recorded among victual rents on some estates in the Garioch
and around Aberdeen but it does not seem to have been a
common crop. Legumes, especially peas, were also sometimes
grown as a field crop. Aberdeenshire suffered from having virtually no local supplies of lime, the fertilizer which had produced a mini-revolution in arable farming in the Lothians during
the early seventeenth century.[8] There it had dramatically improved crop yields, allowing the expansion of more intensively
cultivated infields at the expense of outfields, and encouraging
the intake of new arable land from pasture. In the North East
the limestones of Strathisla in Banffshire were being burnt with
peat to produce agricultural lime in the later seventeenth century.[9] However, although lime from this area was sometimes
transported to the east coast of Aberdeenshire for use as mor-
tar[10] there is no record that it was ever brought in sufficient
quantities for agricultural use. The only limestone outcrop in
Aberdeenshire which was worked for this purpose was one near
Strichen.[11] Seaweed was widely used as a fertilizer in coastal
areas, but inland districts had a very limited choice of fertilizers

to supplement animal manure.

It was probably for this reason that many Aberdeenshire farmers had adopted the pernicious practice of paring turf off the surface of pasture and even poorer arable land, and mixing it with manure to form a compost for their infields, sometimes applying 700 cartloads per acre. That this did no good to the land in the long term was widely appreciated. In 1683 for instance the baron court of Rubislaw forbade tenants to dig turf for making 'muck middens'.[12] In 1685 the Scottish parliament tackled the problem by passing an act to encourage the sowing of peas as an alternative way of improving the soil.[13] Aberdeenshire was specifically mentioned as an area where farmers commonly dug turf in this way. It is doubtful if sowing peas in the small quantities specified in the act would have had much effect but the national legislation was echoing the efforts of local proprietors, through their baron courts, to spread the use of legumes whose nitrogen-fixing properties were appreciated though not understood. In 1671 the Forbes baron court stipulated that every unit of land paying 100 merks or a chalder of meal in rent should have two pecks of peas sown on it.[14] The burgh of Banff had passed a similar resolution relating to its lands in 1659.[15] After 1685 baron courts could quote the parliamentary act to lend authority to their rulings, and they did so frequently. The small quantities of peas which they expected farmers to sow suggests, however, that they were often sown only on a few infield rigs rather than forming a full course as was common further south.

Aberdeenshire estate papers provide some examples of improved crop rotation. Rotations of bere/oats/peas rather than the traditional bere/oats/oats is recorded from some estates;[16] so is the insertion of a fallow course into the unbroken succession of cereals on the infield.[17] Where wheat was grown it was added to a rotation of bere and oats and, as it was regarded as an exhausting crop, it was preceded by either a fallow course or a crop of peas.[18] The supposedly 'typical' rotations of bere followed by two crops of oats do occur but so do rotations with only one and as many as three crops of oats between bere. Outfield rotations are even less frequently recorded but examples show that three or four crops of oats were generally taken before the outfield was rested and that a fallow of four to five years was normal.[19] The problem is, of course, that such reference are sporadic. They may not be representative and do not give us any idea of how much, or how little local variation occurred.

What yields did these rotations produce? Information on yields is as difficult to obtain as data on rotations. Generally one can only calculate them from the accounts of estate mains where the quantities of grain sown and harvested are given. However, Garden of Troup's observation that infield yields in the north of the shire could go as high as five or six to one but were often closer to four to one is in line with information from other parts of Scotland.[20] On outfield land the first crop after fallow might give as high as six or seven to one in exceptional cases. Such yields, while not spectacular, were at least an improvement on the break-even yield of three to one which is often assumed to have been normal.

A category of arable land which did not fit into the standard framework of infield-outfield farming was known as 'burntland'. This resulted from the practice of ditching the surface of the ground around the edge of a peat moss, paring off the dried-out surface layer, piling it into heaps, burning it and sowing a crop in the ashes. The cropping of burntland was widespread in Aberdeenshire; its attraction was that yields of up to seventeen or twenty to one could be obtained because of the rich mineral content of the ash layer.[21] Unfortunately, if the practice was long continued, it could lead to a shortage of peat as the moss gradually became burnt out. The court book of Leys in 1649 referred to scarcity of peat mosses on the estate due to the 'great abuse of burning them and making bruntland'.[22] The baillie recorded that henceforth tenants were not to cultivate any land in this manner without the express permission of the laird. In 1671 the factor at Belhelvie was recorded patrolling the proprietor's peat mosses to check whether any tenants had been encroaching on them in this way.[23]

### Enclosure and improved farming

We should visualize Aberdeenshire farming at this time taking place in a landscape which was mainly open, unenclosed and treeless. Enclosures were confined to the policies surrounding the country houses of the landowners, and even here the scale was limited compared with more progressive parts of Scotland. From the mid seventeenth century a fashion had developed for rebuilding or extending old fortified houses and laying out more extensive policies around them.[24] This trend had been encouraged by parliamentary legislation granting tax concessions on enclosed land for plantations of trees and also for agriculture. Activity was greatest in south east Scotland and also in Galloway where it was linked to the profitable cattle trade with

England. Late seventeenth and early eighteenth century descriptions of Aberdeenshire make only sporadic references to such enclosures, in contrast with neighbouring areas like Forfarshire. These references relate mainly to the planting of trees. Much of this was on a very small scale but at Kildrummy, for example, the planted timber in 1703 amounted to over 13,000 trees,[25] limited compared with the millions of trees said to have been planted far later in the century for Sir Archibald Grant of Monymusk[26] but nevertheless a significant development. Most of the lowlands of Aberdeenshire had been stripped of their woodlands long before the seventeenth century, and only the pine and birch woods at the head of the Dee remained. Even these were under threat. A factor's report to the earl of Mar in 1707[27] suggested that the value of the earl's pinewoods around Braemar had risen because the woods of Glentanar, closer to the main centres of population, were becoming worked out due to large-scale felling and lack of replanting. Inadequate management by ordinary people, who cut green timber whenever they could, despite innumerable acts passed by baron courts,[28] lay at the heart of the problem. Planting and enclosure had to go hand in hand because of the need to protect the young trees from livestock in an open landscape. Under the circumstances it was inevitable that the initiative came from the landowners and not their tenants. The planting of woods around country houses was done for ornamental purposes, but there was also an economic side to it; timber was valuable and represented a reserve of capital which could be drawn on if an estate came into financial difficulties. The later seventeenth century saw the birth of modern commercial forestry in Aberdeenshire. As early as the 1680s a start had been made in trying to encourage the tenantry to plant and protect trees. Leases on the Gordon estates at this time began to contain clauses requiring tenants to plant a certain number of trees each year on their farms — up to twenty — and protect them or face penalties.[29]

Enclosures round country houses also allowed proprietors to experiment with new methods of farming before trying to disseminate them more widely. This was the course followed by Grant of Monymusk and other improvers in the first half of the eighteenth century.[30] It is not clear whether Grant was the first Aberdeenshire landowner to introduce better rotations and new  crops such as sown grasses and turnips. He may merely have got the credit for it. Certainly, the accounts for a number of estates in the county show that in the late seventeenth century their parks and mains were being managed with increasing attention to efficiency. At Gordon Castle large numbers of cattle were bought from the tenants and fattened on the controlled and protected grazing within the castle's parks.[31] The pace of progress, even in the eighteenth century, was indoubtedly slow and it took a long time for enclosure to spread beyond the mains to the tenants' farms. This was partly due to lack of capital investment by landlords and tenant alike. However, so much of the credit for initiating agricultural improvement has traditionally gone to the landowners that it is easy to underestimate the contribution of the ordinary farmers. Much of the enclosure on the Monymusk estates, for example, was not done by hired labourers working for Grant himself, but by his tenants, who received a reduction in rent but did the work themselves, and must presumably have been sufficiently enthusiastic about it to take leases offered on these terms.[32] The Military Survey of 1747-55 shows how little enclosure had been achieved by the middle of the eighteenth century. Nevertheless, a start had been made in preparing the rural population for the changes to come. From the 1680s tacks on the Gordon estates began to include clauses stipulating that tenants were to be compensated for any improvements such as ditching and dyke making which they carried out.[33] This does not, of course, prove that they actually undertook improvements but it did remove one obstacle to their doing so, namely the fear that any such efforts would bring no benefit to the tenant if he removed at the end of a short lease.

### Market centres

In the seventeenth century Aberdeenshire was not highly urbanised compared with areas further south. Indeed, although Aberdeen was one of the largest regional centres in Scotland, the North East was poorly provided with smaller burghs possessing a wide range of crafts and services. The poll tax lists of 1696 show that only Fraserburgh and Peterhead were large enough to act as major sub-regional centres. Old royal burghs like Inverurie and Kintore were very small and were barely distinguishable in size or function from the rural kirktouns. Figure 2 shows the distribution of market centres within the county in 1600 — assuming that all the baronial burghs which had been authorised by parliament were actually functioning. It also shows those areas which were within easy range of existing centres. The distance bands are arbitrary but they do show that much of Buchan and large areas in the west of the county were distant from market centres.

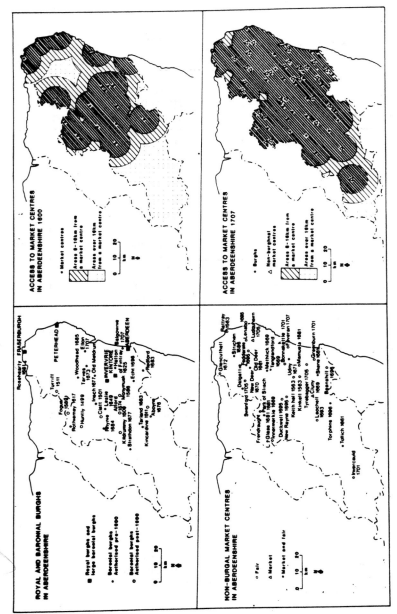

Figure 2 Market centres in Aberdeenshire in the 17th and early 18 centuries

During the seventeenth century many new market centres were authorised in Aberdeenshire as elsewhere in Scotland. Some were new burghs of barony but after 1660 new centres, authorised to hold markets and fairs but without burgh status were created (Figure 2). The establishment of these new centres reflects a move away from the medieval system of burghal monopolies which was becoming restrictive and unworkable. It is difficult to know to what extent this rash of new foundations was designed to encourage the growth of local trade, or to cream off revenue from existing unofficial trade by creating more outlets where tolls could be charged.[34] Overall, however, the provision of market centres was greatly improved during the later seventeenth century. Figure 2 shows that by 1707 the county was much more effectively served than a century earlier and that virtually no part of the county was more than sixteen kilometres from a market centre.

The initiative behind the establishment of these new market centres came not from central government but from local landowners. Although there was a pause between the authorisation of the last of these market centres in the early eighteenth century and the foundation of the first planned estate villages in the 1750s and 1760s, the latter were nonetheless a continuation of the earlier tradition, often on adjacent sites, modified to meet changing economic circumstances. The seventeenth century market centres were designed to improve trade; fostering domestic industry was a secondary consideration. Many of the planned villages were designed to promote linen and woollen manufacturing but they often acted as local service centres too.[35]

The new market centres of the seventeenth century did not usually require any great outlay of capital by the landowners who promoted them, particularly the non-burghal ones where markets and fairs were generally attached to existing kirktouns, requiring no more facilities than a suitable piece of open ground. Some landowners did invest capital in their new foundations; this was particularly the case with coastal burghs of barony like Fraserburgh, where Sir Alexander Fraser of Philorth had to provide breakwaters to create a safe harbour and encourage trade.[36]

## Trade

While Aberdeenshire farming at this period cannot be considered as highly commercialised, the marked regional variations in agriculture within the county generated trade of necessity. In every area the inhabitants tried to produce as much of their basic needs as possible but complete self sufficiency was rarely possible. The uplands were perenially short of grain, the lowlands looked to the hills for their horses, cattle and oxen. The burghs, especially Aberdeen, required a steady flow of agricultural produce from their surrounding hinterlands to sustain their populations. In addition the county regularly produced agricultural surpluses for sale outside the region. The surpluses produced by individual tenants after they had paid their rents and set aside their requirements for food and seed were often limited. Their involvement in trade was strictly small scale, through local market centres. Most of the bulk trade was in the hands of the landowners who received large quantities of grain and other produce in rents. Aberdeenshire was not as large an exporter of grain as some parts of eastern Scotland. The port books for the customs precinct centred on Aberdeen show, for instance, that in the bumper harvest year of 1684-5 the Aberdeen precinct came only eighth, exporting barely a sixth as much grain as the Montrose and Dundee precincts.[37] One reason for this may have been that much of lowland Aberdeenshire's surplus of grain was traded into the Highlands which were always short of cereals. The accounts for the Gordon estates around Huntly in the late seventeenth and early eighteenth centuries show that large quantities of grain were regularly sold to 'the men of Badenoch'.[38]

Much of the agricultural surplus of areas like Buchan left Aberdeen in the form of knitted hosiery and webs of coarse woollen plaiding, for which the town was Scotland's major exporter. In some Buchan parishes nearly a fifth of the adult males in the poll tax lists of 1696 were described as weavers[39] (Figure 3). The cloth was bought by Aberdeen merchants who travelled from one local fair to another. The cattle trade was also flourishing in the late seventeenth century. Larger landowners could buy in lean stock and fatten them in their parks for resale. Tenants too could enter the trade on a small scale by buying in extra animals or by taking other farmers' livestock on to the summer pastures for a fee. A factor's report for the earl of Mar's estates on upper Deeside early in the eighteenth century showed that tenants and feuars of the earl were taking lowland cattle with their own animals to the summer shielings.[40] These were becoming overstocked as a result and new shielings were being pushed higher into the earl's deer forests. Efforts to restrict this practice seem to have been unsuccessful and in some areas, like Glenrinnes, south east of Dufftown. the proprietors merely acquiesced to it and set about finding ways of

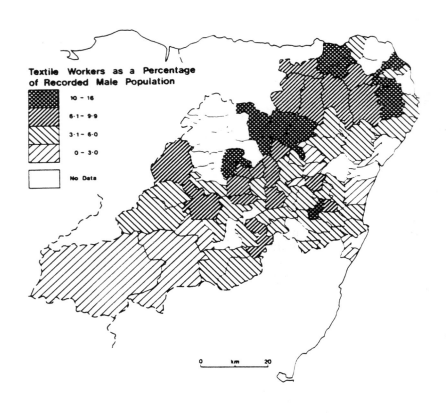

Textile Workers as a Percentage
of Recorded Male Population

10 - 16
6·1 - 9·9
3·1 - 6·0
0 - 3·0
No Data

0        km        20

Figure 3

Rent  Lowland = Grain Cattle
                Poultry Cloth,
                peat eggs.

      Uplands    money, - Strange
                why - produce easily
                marketed
                Cloth - Cattle on the herf

extracting some of the profit from the tenants as extra rent.[41]

## Rent

An important element of continuity from the seventeenth century into the eighteenth was the form in which rents were paid. Most lowland tenants paid the main part of their rent in grain, generally ground oatmeal and bere. They were also liable for small payments of a variety of produce to maintain their landlord and his household. An old rental of the Lordship of Huntly in 1600 required that most of the tenants pay marts — cattle for slaughter and salting at Martinmas — as well as wethers, lambs, geese, ducks, grouse, hens, eggs, linen cloth, straw and loads of peat.[42] Tenants in such areas often had to undertake labour services as well. These could include ploughing, harrowing, carting manure and harvesting on the mains, using their own animals and equipment. They also cut and carried peat for the landowner, and took their grain rents to market. The survival of such rents emphasises that although Aberdeenshire tenants were legally free men their relationship with their landlord still held an important element of feudalism. These antiquated rents had not been abolished and converted to money for two main reasons — the commercial element in the economy was not yet sufficiently strong for this to be a viable proposition, while at the same time the retention of these rents undoubtedly limited the tenants' participation in the market economy and slowed the progress of more commercial attitudes. This explains why the bulk of the grain trade was in the landowners' hands.

It was mainly in the upland and semi-upland areas that principal rents in money were found. The existence of money rents in these remote areas, furthest from the commercial influences of the burghs, might seem strange. It probably stemmed in part from the difficulties of farmers in such areas in discharging labour services when the proprietor's castle or mansion was distant. Also, the pastoral products of such areas were more easily marketable, on the hoof in the case of livestock and as high value, low weight commodities like wool, instead of bulky grain.

There was some progress in the commutation of rents in kind to money payments during the seventeenth and early eighteenth centuries, but the pace of change was slow. Small payments in kind were often the first to go, as with more peaceful conditions landowners tended to reduce their households doing away with the large bodies of retainers they had once accommodated, finding as a result that they had excess produce on their hands. There was less progress in converting grain rents to money partly because the existing system seemed to work well enough. Even at Monymusk Sir Archibald Grant only gradually reduced the victual rent, from 980 bolls in 1733 to 347 in 1767.[43] Services too were only commuted slowly — at Monymusk Grant's improving activities actually generated a greater demand for the carriage services of the tenants in hauling stone, lime and other commodities.[44]

### Farm and holding structures

The traditional idea of the Scottish pre-improvement farm is one in which a number of tenants (four, six, eight or sometimes more) held shares, working in cooperation. Their lands were intermingled in a system known as runrig which resulted from the need to divide the shares in a farm with strict regard to the quality as well as the quantity of land. This required that the best and the worst land should be shared, producing fragment-ation into scattered strips and blocks. The holdings worked by such tenants were generally too small to provide them with more than a bare subsistence. More detailed research has shown that while this view was not totally inaccurate, reality was more complex. This can be seen from the 1696 poll tax records[45] and sets of estate rentals. These show that while multiple-tenant farms existed, large farms leased by single tenants and worked mainly by cottars, who sublet small portions of land, and by living in farm servants, were dominant in many areas. Farms of this kind accounted for 70% or more of all farms over much of Buchan, the Garioch and the area around Aberdeen (Figure 4). By contrast, in the upper reaches of the Don and Dee, multiple-tenant farms with up to twelve joint farmers and few cottars or servants were usual. Why did such contrasts occur? In the up-lands where only small areas were cultivated for subsistence and the main resources of a farm were its grazings, the inefficiencies resulting from multiple, fragmented occupancy of the limited areas of arable did not matter greatly. In the lowlands, however, where grain was the product which paid the rent, it was more efficient to work the arable land in larger units using hired labour. This is a simplification of course because one can find examples of neighbouring estates, with most of the farms on one in single-tenancy and on the other in multiple-tenancy, em-phasising the importance of an individual landowner's decision-making.

The implication is, nevertheless, that single-tenancy was

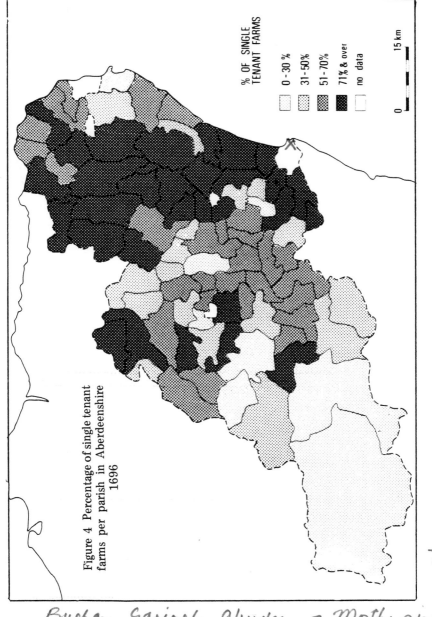

% OF SINGLE
TENANT FARMS

0 - 30 %
31 - 50%
51 - 70%
71% & over
no data

0                15 km

Figure 4 Percentage of single tenant
farms per parish in Aberdeenshire
1696

x A/Deen

Buchan Garioch aberdeen. = Mostly single
                                        tenants

Upper Dee and Don — many joint tenants.

more commercially efficient for an arable-oriented farm provided that tenants could be found with the resources to stock the larger units. Where rentals from the sixteenth and early seventeenth century are available for comparison with late seventeenth century ones, the pattern is one of gradual reduction in the numbers of shares on multiple-tenant farms, with eventual consolidation to single-tenancy.[46] This process was far from complete by the early eighteenth century, but the slow change towards a more efficient type of farm structure was important. Apart from indicating changes in landlord policy representing the first move towards a more commercial system, another factor behind this evolution may have been increasing prosperity among certain sectors of the tenantry allowing them to stock and work larger farms. In parts of Aberdeenshire this trend may have been linked to growing profits from the cattle trade.

These geographical contrasts, and gradual changes, in farm organisation had important implications for the structure of rural society. In Strathdon and the upper Dee the rural population was not markedly differentiated. Tenants, mostly small ones, formed over 40% of the active population in some parishes in 1696. By contrast, in many lowland areas, where larger single-tenant farms dominated, the proportion of tenants in the active population was something under 10% (Figure 5). In parishes such as these rural society was becoming split into a smaller class of tenants who were becoming more distinctly separated in wealth and status from the growing body of cottars and farm servants. The trend towards creating fewer and larger holdings was, in the long term, one of the most important influences on rural society. Continuing through the eighteenth century it produced a class of more prosperous farmers who were able to take advantage of incentives to improvement offered by their landlord, and by the developing market economy, people who were able to invest capital and were willing to invest labour in enclosure and drainage. In this way we can see the evolution of the capitalist farmer of the nineteenth century starting in the seventeenth century. Over the same period an increasingly large proportion of the rural population became stuck within the cottar class with less chance of upward mobility. As holding consolidation increased it became harder to break into the tenantry from below, to raise the capital to stock a farm, unless you inherited. When the cottars became deprived of their small stakes in the land in the interests of greater farming efficiency, towards the end of the eighteenth century, they evolved into the landless group of wage-earning ploughmen and labourers

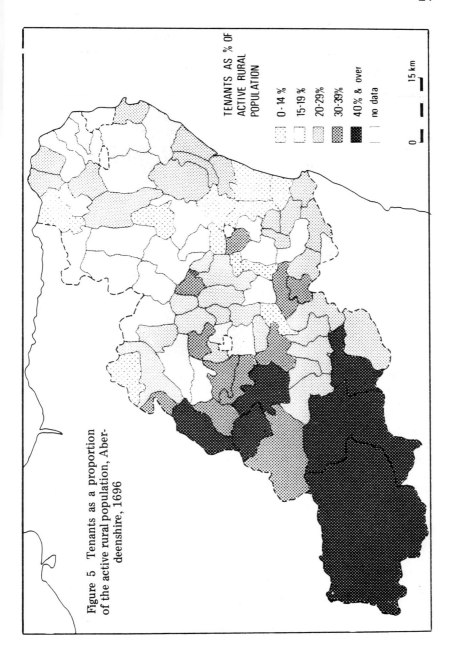

Figure 5 Tenants as a proportion of the active rural population, Aberdeenshire, 1696

TENANTS AS % OF ACTIVE RURAL POPULATION

0 - 14 %
15-19 %
20-29%
30-39%
40% & over
no data

0        15 km

who are so familiar in later times.

The tenant farmers were not necessarily a homogeneous group in the seventeenth and early eighteenth centuries however. Examination of estate rentals shows that in most areas there was a good deal of variation in holding sizes. But rentals and other sources rarely give the actual acreage of a holding: they may express size as a traditional assessment in ploughgates — the amount of land which a ploughteam, nominally of eight oxen, could keep in cultivation — or in other ways. The problem is to know how much land these assessements actually meant. A ploughgate in Aberdeenshire was often reckoned to extend to some eighty Scots acres but this included outfield as well as infield. Given that the outfield formed the greater proportion of the arable land and that much of it was in fallow at any time, a farm might only have half or less of its arable in cultivation in any year. Many farmers with half a ploughgate or less may have depended on under twenty acres of cropland to support them. A high proportion of tenants on many estates may then have been close to the margins of subsistence.

This is confirmed from the lists of rent arrears which are a perennial feature of estate accounts. After a bad year tenants who could not pay their rent would not necessarily be evicted. There was still a good deal of paternalism in landowners' attitudes, and more practically, there was little point in removing a tenant at a difficult time when there might be little hope of finding a more suitable man to take his place. As a result tenants often stayed put and accumulated a burden of debt. On farms where the rent was paid in grain the problem was exacerbated by the system of recording arrears as a money equivalent based on the high market prices of a year of shortage, possibly two or three times the normal level. Tenants then had to pay these off from the modest surpluses of good years when grain prices were low. Larger tenants were in a better position to clear such debt because their surpluses were larger and they had more flexibility in their operations.

The retention of this system shows clearly the lack of long-term planning and the pursuit of short-term expediency in landowners' thinking. Most holdings were probably rented too highly in relation to their productivity and as a result it was hard for farmers, especially small ones, to accumulate capital. This perpetuated the wide social gulf between landlord and tenant. Landlords were not averse to borrowing money from their tenants but ordinary farmers rarely accumulated enough money to acquire land on a permanent basis.

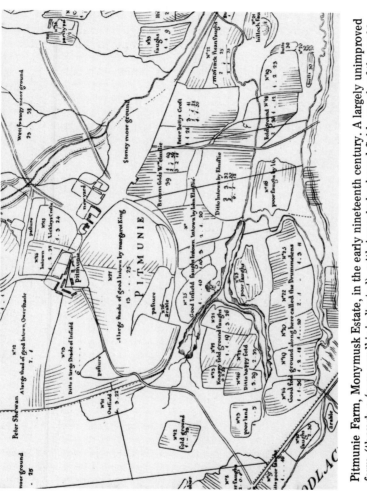

Pitmunie Farm, Monymusk Estate, in the early nineteenth century. A largely unimproved farm (though a 'new yard' is indicated), with irregularly shaped fields, much of the arable land still divided into 'runrig' strips held by different tenants, and tenants' houses grouped together to form a 'ferm toun'.

Mains of Monymusk Farm in 1774. An improved farm, with straight-edged fields separated from each other by dykes and sometimes belts of trees forming windbreaks. The straight new roads are also lined with trees, and poor land has been afforested. Like many improving landlords Sir Archibald Grant of Monymusk began improvement on the mains, the home farm, and comprehensive improvement might take many years to reach outlying farms — as the much later plan of Pitmunie, on the same estate, indicates.

The structure of rents and holdings, along with the limitations of agricultural techniques, rendered farmers vulnerable to the effects of bad harvests. This was graphically demonstrated during the famines of the later 1690s. We do not know the full story of this, the last great subsistence crisis to affect North Eastern Scotland, but parish registers, rentals and other sources provide some detail. There were major contrasts within Aberdeenshire in the effects of the famine. In lowland areas while tenants often built up spectacular levels of arrears they rarely starved. At Belhelvie, north of Aberdeen, the turnover of tenants during the famine years was actually lower than normal — presumably because there was nowhere better to go and the factor was unwilling to let tenants leave with a backlog of arrears.[47] Mortality in Belhelvie parish during the crisis years rose substantially, but the casualties were the cottars and smallholders rather than the larger farmers.

The story was undoubtedly worse in the upland west of the county. It is here that we find examples of abandoned farms and starving tenants. In areas like the Cabrach tenants were dying of starvation in 1697 and 1698 and their holdings had not been let five years later.[48] Around Huntly in 1705 inducements were being offered to people who would take on untenanted farms. Conditions were more serious in such areas because the crop failures were more disastrous in a marginal upland setting, and the bad weather also caused heavy livestock mortality.[49] It is worth remembering though that this was the last real famine in the North East and that it was the only one in the century between 1650 and 1750. This in itself shows that at this period agriculture in Aberdeenshire was able to feed the population and provide a surplus for export except under exceptional circumstances.

It has only been possible to review here some aspects of farming in Aberdeenshire during the seventeenth and early eighteenth centuries. In this area gradual changes occurred in farming practices and farm organisation, against a background of continuity in the basic framework of agrarian life. Many of the measures taken by the first improvers in the mid eighteenth century had already been tried in the seventeenth, such as attempts to persuade tenants to plant trees, refrain from paring off turf for manure, sow legumes, and restrict the number of crops which they took from their outfields. It took more favourable economic conditions after the middle of the eighteenth century with growing population and rising standards of living leading to higher food prices for them to be fully adopted.

Nevertheless, many of the changes in the organisation of agriculture such as the reduction of multiple tenancies, and the commutation of rents in kind had begun in the seventeenth century and accelerated gradually through the eighteenth. In presenting this picture of the slowly changing character of Aberdeenshire farming the intention has been to highlight those aspects about which we know something and to pinpoint topics on which our knowledge is very incomplete in order to back up generalisations by detailed studies of particular communities at the scale of the estate or parish to see how the gradual changes which have been outlined here affected the ordinary people of the county.

REFERENCES

1   J.E. Handley, *Scottish farming in the eighteenth century* (Edinburgh, 1953) and *The agricultural revolution in Scotland* (Edinburgh, 1963).
2   E. Kerridge, *The agricultural revolution* (London, 1967).
3   I.D. Whyte, *Agriculture and Society in seventeenth-century Scotland* (Edinburgh, 1979).
4   Description of eighteen parishes in the shire and diocese of Aberdeen in *Macfarlane's Geographical Collections*, ed. A. Mitchell (3 vols. Scottish History Society, 1906-8), i, 19-36.
5   For an indication of how these can be used see I.D. Whyte and K.A. Whyte, 'Regional and local variations in seventeenth-century Scottish farming: a preliminary survey of the evidence of commissary court testaments', *Manchester Geographer*, 3 (1983), 49-59.
6   J. Anderson, *General view of the agriculture of the county of Aberdeen* (Edinburgh, 1794).
7   J. Wilson, 'Farming in Aberdeenshire, ancient and modern', *Transactions of the Highland and Agricultural Society* (1902), 72.
8   Whyte, *Agriculture and society*, 198-208.
9   *Macfarlane's Geographical Collections*, i, 74, 75, 82.
10  Ibid., i, 60.
11  Scottish Record Office (hereafter SRO), Haddo muniments, GD. 33/30/49.
12  SRO, Skene of Rubislaw muniments GD. 244/4, Tack 1683.
13  *Acts of the Parliaments of Scotland*, viii, 484.
14  *Miscellany of the Scottish History Society*, iii (1919), 283.
15  W. Cramond (ed.), *The annals of Banff* (2 vols, Spalding Club, 1891-3), ii, 141.
16  SRO, Skene of Rubislaw muniments GD. 244/4, Tack 1668.

17  SRO, Gordon muniments, GD. 44/20/10.
18  Ibid., GD. 44/51/747.
19  SRO, Dalhousie muniments, GD 45/20/51.
20  A. Garden Troup, 'An account of the northside of the coast of Buchan', in *Macfarlane's Geographical Collections*, ii, 139.
21  Ibid., ii, 141. Lady Anne Drummond, 'An account of Buchan and what is remarkable therein', in *Collections for a history of the shires of Aberdeen and Banff* (Spalding Club, 1843), 95.
22  'Extracts from the court book of the barony of Leys', in *Miscellany*, v (Spalding Club, 1852), 229.
23  SRO, Dalhousie muniments, GD. 45/20/14.
24  Whyte, *Agriculture and society*, 113-32.
25  SRO, Mar and Kellie muniments, GD. 124/17/102.
26  H. Hamilton (ed.), *Selections from the Monymusk papers 1713-55* (Scottish History Society, 1945), xlviii-xlix.
27  SRO, Mar and Kellie muniments GD. 124/17/102.
28  'Court book of Leys', 222.
29  SRO, Gordon muniments, GD. 44/17/27, 44/18/25, 44/18/29, 44/19/3, 44/19/10, 44/19/11, 44/19/12 (tacks).
30  Hamilton, *Monymusk papers*, lxvi ff.
31  SRO, Gordon muniments, GD. 44/51/25, 44/51/74, 44/51/75.
32  Hamilton, *Monymusk papers*, 19-51.
33  SRO, Gordon muniments, tacks as cited in n. 29 above.
34  I.D. Whyte, 'The growth of periodic market centres in Scotland 1600-1707', *Scottish Geographical Magazine*, 95 (1979), 13-26.
35  D.G. Lockhart, The evolution of the planned villages of North East Scotland: studies in settlement geography. (Unpublished Ph.D. thesis, University of Dundee, 1974).
36  Ibid., 256.
37  Whyte, *Agriculture and society*, 232.
38  SRO, Gordon muniments, GD. 44/51/25, 44/51/74, 44/51/75 (accounts).
39  J. Stuart (ed.), *List of pollable persons in the shire of Aberdeen 1696* (2 vols., Aberdeen, 1844).
40  SRO, Mar and Kellie muniments, GD. 124/17/202.
41  SRO, Gordon muniments, GD. 44/51/739 (rental).
42  Ibid., GD. 44/51/747.
43  Hamilton, *Monymusk papers*, lxxiv.
44  Ibid., 45.
45  Stuart, *List of pollable persons*.
46  Whyte, *Agriculture and society*, 156.
47  SRO, Dalhousie muniments, GD 45/20 (estate rentals).
48  SRO, Gordon muniments, GD. 44/51/740.
49  Ibid.

# FAMINE IN ABERDEENSHIRE, 1695–1699: ANATOMY OF A CRISIS

## ROBERT E. TYSON

Recent events in Africa have made us only too aware of the consequences of famine, which may be defined as a shortage of food so severe that it causes widespread mortality either as a result of starvation or starvation-related diseases. The suffering appears all the more terrible because it is so unfamiliar; the problem in the developed countries of the world today is not too little food but too much. Apart from the period of the two World Wars, there has been no famine in Western Europe since the 1840s when the failure of the potato crop hit Ireland so badly, and this was exceptional. Most European countries had conquered famine during the eighteenth century, while in England it was no longer a serious problem after 1630. In Scotland the last major famine occurred during the 1690s, a decade in which there was starvation on a massive scale in a number of European countries.[1]

Contemporaries referred to this period in Scotland as 'the seven ill years', 'King William's dear years' or 'the black years of King William' (particularly if they were Jacobites). However, as Professor Smout has shown, the crisis lasted in most areas from the harvest of 1695 to that of 1700 and not all years were equally bad; there were usually three years of high mortality out of the five, so the title of 'the seven lean years' is an exaggeration. Moreover, the famine varied in its severity between one region and another. The West of Scotland, partly because of its proximity to Ireland which offered supplies of food and a refuge to the hungry, was probably the least hit region, and the Highlands the worst.[2] Within the North East a later account stated that 'the province of Murray and some of the best lands along the east coast of Buchan and Formartine abounded with feed and bread', while further inland the population of Monquhitter fell by half or more.[3] Overall, however, it seems quite likely that Aberdeenshire experienced a mortality crisis that was exceptional even by the standards of the pre-industrial period, and may have been more severe than anywhere in Scotland except the Highlands.

The main cause of the crisis was the impact of bad weather

on successive harvests and therefore on food prices. During the first five years of the 1690s the price of farm meal, the staple food of most of the population, averaged £4 Scots a boll and this included the bad harvest of 1690 when it reached £5.6.8d Scots (see Table 1. £12 Scots = £1 sterling). Because of wet weather, however, the harvest of 1695 was so bad that the price of oatmeal eventually doubled during the next twelve months to reach £8 Scots a boll. A second bad harvest then followed, and although that of 1697 was gathered under fairly good conditions, there was no reduction in price. The Aberdeenshire fiar courts at this period met in February or March and August. In normal years there was no difference between the two prices struck but during the famine the August one was always much the higher; this reflected prices at a time when grain was likely to be scarce and when the prospect of another bad harvest would become apparent, although any harvest, however bad, would offer some relief. The worst harvest of all, however, was that of 1698. Previous bad harvests had resulted in a shortage of seed-corn (normally a quarter of the crop was retained for this purpose but in times of famine, when the proportion should have risen to a third or even a half because of the reduced yield, much of the seed-corn would be consumed) while cold weather in spring delayed germination. Most damage in 1698, however, was done at harvest time when there were winds, rain and snow. Some of the corn was cut as late as January 1699, and much was never harvested at all. A similar harvest in 1782, after making provision for seed-corn, produced little more than a quarter of the usual amount of meal.[4] The February 1699 price of £10.13.4d was actually higher than that just before the harvest while that in August reached £13.6.8d, the highest recorded before the end of the eighteenth century when the general price level was much higher; it is likely that the actual market price rose even more. Although harvest conditions in 1699 were good, particularly for oats, the price of meal was still double that before 1695, probably because so much ground remained unsown for want of seed-corn and work oxen, and it was not until the autumn of 1700 that prices at last fell back to their pre-crisis level.

It is generally agreed that from the middle of the sixteenth century onwards there was a worsening of the weather throughout Europe which is usually referred to as 'the little ice age'. The movement south of Artic sea-ice produced colder winters and cooler, wetter summers. It has been estimated that at the climax of the little ice-age in the 1690s, the annual mean

## TABLE 1

*Fiar price of a boll of farm meal: Aberdeenshire*

| Harvest year | Price (£ Scots) | Date of court | |
|---|---|---|---|
| 1690-4 (av.) | £ 4. 0.0. | March and August 1691-5 | |
| 1695 | £ 5. 6.8 | March | 1696 |
| 1695 | £ 8. 0.0 | August | 1696 |
| 1696 | £ 6. 0.0 | March | 1697 |
| 1696 | £ 8. 0.0. | August | 1697 |
| 1697 | £ 6.13.4 | March | 1698 |
| 1697 | £ 8. 0.0 | August | 1698 |
| 1698 | £10.13.4 | February | 1699 |
| 1698 | £13. 6.8 | August | 1699 |
| 1699 | £ 8. 0.0 | March | 1700 |
| 1699 | £ 8. 0.0 | August | 1700 |
| 1700-4 (av.) | £ 4.14.4 | February and March 1701-6 | |

Source: David Littlejohn (ed.), 'Aberdeenshire Fiars', 20-3, in P.J. Anderson (ed.), *Miscellany of the New Spalding Club* (Aberdeen, 1908), ii.

temperature in England was 1.5° centigrade lower than the mean between 1920 and 1960 and May 1698 was the coldest ever recorded there. However, since the water surface off the Northern Isles may have been 4-5° centigrade colder than the mean of the last hundred years, the reduction in the air temperature of North East Scotland must have been considerably greater than in England and much of Scotland. This probably explains travellers' references in this period to permanent snows on the tops of the Cairngorms and lochans covered with ice during the summer months and would suggest temperatures 2-2.5° centigrade lower than in 1920-60.[5] Such a reduction would have a serious effect on the germination and ripening of crops in low-lying areas but the consequences for the upland and highland parts of Aberdeenshire would have been much worse, since the chances of a bad harvest increase very rapidly with altitude.[6] One would expect, therefore, the damage caused by bad weather to have been much greater there than in the lowlands, and for Aberdeenshire as a whole to fare much worse than more favoured areas of Scotland.

It is increasingly recognised, however, that famine was not simply the result of bad harvests though this was clearly the most important cause. Few pre-industrial societies, let alone a relatively poor one like Aberdeenshire, could have withstood the impact of a succession of bad years without heavy loss of life but other factors combined to make the crisis even worse.

Aberdeenshire in this period was a major producer of coarse woollen cloth (plaids) and stockings which were largely made in rural areas, particularly in a broad belt of parishes which stretched westwards from the Buchan coast to Strathbogie. In some parishes here a fifth or more of the adult males listed in the 1695 Poll Book had trades, 60 per cent of them as weavers and shoemakers.[7] The Poll Book does not give the occupations of women but the proportion engaged in spinning and knitting was probably much greater. Some tradesmen were also tenants but the great majority were sub-tenants, cottars and grassmen, or had no land at all. Such people were clearly dependent upon their trades for part or even all of their livelihood; to quote a contemporary account of Buchan, it was the manufacture of the plaids and stockings 'which bringeth money to the commons, other ways of getting it they have not'.[8] A bad harvest meant that they had to spend proportionately more of this money on food at a time when high prices caused their customers both at home and abroad to purchase less cloth and fewer stockings.

The problem of these and other Aberdeenshire exports, however, was made much more acute by the consequences of the war with France between 1688 and 1697. Exports of cloth from Aberdeen had been in difficulties since at least 1680 but the decline seems to have become really serious from 1694-5 onwards and continued throughout the famine years, so that by 1700 they were little more than half their previous level.[9] This fall in exports, as well as lowering the income of producers and exporters, reduced the ability of Aberdeen to purchase what grain was available abroad, while French privateers roaming off the coast impeded imports.

King William's wars had other consequences, too, notably an increase in taxation at a time when people could least afford it and which drained away cash, always in short supply, to meet the needs of the armed forces. Successive poll taxes and other special taxes, such as the Excise, hit Aberdeen particularly hard since the burgh was still struggling to pay off heavy debts incurred during the Civil War period.[10]

The impact of bad harvests, therefore, was made much worse by the depression in trade and the financial demands of the government in a period of rapidly rising prices. In such circumstances the availability of poor relief could literally mean the difference between life and death and yet at the same time as the kirk sessions needed more and more money to deal with growing numbers of poor, collections and other sources (such as fines for sexual offences) tended to diminish while money lent out on bond to heritors proved difficult or even impossible to recall.

The distribution of poor relief in the North East, however, was made more difficult by the consequences of the religious settlement of 1690, which re-established presbyterianism. A number of ministers, particularly in the Aberdeen area and along the coast, were deposed for episcopalianism and it was not easy to replace them or any other ministers who left during this period. Aberdeenshire had an establishment of ninety ministers at that time but only sixty-one were in office between October 1695 and September 1699, while seventeen parishes had vacancies for a year and four (Aboyne and Glentanar, Kemnay, Old Machar, and Skene) were without ministers throughout the famine.[11] When vacancies did occur, there were sometimes no services, collections or distributions. Old Machar parish had no communions, a valuable source of funds, between 1691 and 1703, while at Foveran the deposed minister recorded in his diary in May 1698 that those starving were unable to receive interest on 600 merks lent out to local heritors because he had retained the bonds.[12]

The amount of money from whatever source at the disposal of a parish was not enough to shield the poor entirely from the impact of famine. In Old Machar those who were judged incapable of supporting themselves — about ninety individuals — normally received a quarterly pension which averaged about fifty shillings a year. Since the average per capita consumption of meal was at least two bolls a year, this sum supplied only a small part of food requirements even when prices were low. There was also a weekly distribution of money to the other poor of the parish and strangers. In the five years before 1695, the average donation was eight shillings and sixpence and few people received more than one. During the famine donations increased five-fold, and the average fell to just over three shillings in 1699. A few parishioners were given money almost every week but none had more than £9 in a year and the great majority of poor received less than £1. Most relief was presumably provided by relations, neighbours, heritors and private charities.[13]

The most sweeping measures to deal with the plight of the poor were taken in Aberdeen itself, where the problem was made much worse by the large number of beggars who moved there from the countryside. Frequent attempts were made to expel them, beginning as early as September 1696, when 'extraeous beggars' were given a fortnight to leave 'and this tolerance is allowed because of the great scarcity'.[14] Shortly afterwards all merchants and tradesmen who refused to make a reasonable weekly contribution to the poor were taxed and the elders and deacons of St Nicholas Church were ordered to list all persons and their condition 'but especially the poor and how and by whom they are served'.[15] As the crisis worsened, further measures were taken which culminated in the 'overtures for the poor' in April 1699. Those receiving monthly pensions were ordered to appear every three months before a committee to explain their circumstances; they were also obliged to attend church regularly and sit on seats reserved for them. Preference was to be given to 'such as have been ... most serviceable and ... honest traders' and wherever possible the poor were to be set to work. There was concern that 'there be not multiplied benefices bestowed upon one and the same person' and no one was allowed to receive money from more than one fund. All those resident in the town for fewer than seven years were to be expelled and every effort was made to keep out strangers; two people were to be appointed for this purpose in each of the town's quarters and a guard set at each gate, while anyone harbouring poor from the countryside was to be punished or fined. It was also agreed 'that some effectual method be taken to keep out the poor begging children and to transport them to where there nativity hath bene'.[16]

Unfortunately, only two lists of those receiving relief in Aberdeen have survived, both from 1697. The first gives the names of 107 men and women who were to be paid monthly pensions averaging just over twenty-four shillings each to keep them from begging. The second consists of 129 men and women of whom fifteen were to receive quarterly pensions averaging nearly £3 and the remainder monthly pensions of just under fourteen shillings.[17] Further aid of a sort was provided here and elsewhere in the form of free burials for the poor and free or subsidised coffins. The latter in Aberdeen were paid out of fines levied by the justice court for sexual misdemeanours and rose from forty-nine in the year 1695-96 (fifty-three if winding sheets are included) to 196 in 1698-99.[18]

The town council also tried to influence the supply, distribution and even the price of food, not always successfully. Apart from the produce of its gardens and the intensively cultivated crofts within its boundaries, Aberdeen was normally dependent upon the remainder of Aberdeenshire for its food. If there was a bad harvest some grain would be imported from Orkney, the Moray Firth area and Angus, while in times of famine some would also be purchased from England and Danzig. It is clear from the accounts of the St Nicholas 'met' which was levied on shipments of grain and salt that there was a substantial increase in arrivals of the former into Aberdeen despite complaints of a shortage of shipping. In the five years before Michaelmas 1695, shipments averaged less than two a year, but in the year 1698-9 they reached thirty-one.[19] There is no indication of the actual quantities and some grain was probably intended for the remainder of Aberdeenshire but it is likely that most shipments were for consumption in Aberdeen itself.

In July 1696, the town council commissioned Alexander Kerr of Menie to buy 500 bolls of wheat. Kerr, who described 'the meaner sort ... being reduced to very great straits through the scarcity and dearth of victual and several of them ... starving in the streets', could find no supplies until he reached Newcastle and Stockton-on-Tees where he managed to buy wheat, barley, oats and beans. On his way back he put in at Leith and informed the Aberdeen magistrates of what he had done. 'And the prices in this country being then (by the blessing of God) fallen lower', they instructed him to sell the food there, which he did at a loss, including expenses, of £712.12.8d.[20] Within a few months of this misplaced optimism, John Wright, tacksman of the custom levied on sales of meal at the Aberdeen mercat, complained that he was expected to find £710 but had collected only £27 between Whitsunday and October, so scarce was grain.[21] The council declared that some citizens were buying up meal within the town to enhance the price and ordered that all malt coming into the burgh should be sold at the malt mercat and not taken directly to private houses.[22] During the next few years Kerr and Baillie Thomas Mitchell bought meal on behalf of the council which was sold at comparatively low prices in small amounts, usually a peck, which was the average weekly consumption for one person.[23] The quantities bought, however, were small compared with the town's requirements of about 16,000 bolls a year and most meal was probably bought at the full price. The Aberdeen meal mercat, in fact, appears to have collapsed at the height of the famine for in May 1699 it was claimed that anyone with money to buy a firlot of meal went into the countryside to find it.[24] Grain was available, particularly in the coastal parishes such as Belhevie, but at very high prices.[25]

As prices rose, there was a greater reliance on cheaper food-stuffs such as oatmeal, peas and beans (which explains why the more expensive wheat rose less in price than oats) but even before the crisis the majority of people were probably too near the margin of subsistence for this to have much effect. Many were eventually reduced to eating flour made from the wild mustard seed, 'runches' or wild radishes, and nettles.[26] For those in the countryside who were most at risk — the recipients of poor relief, the numerous spinsters and widows, servants dismissed by their employers in order to save food, wage-earners and tradesmen, sub-tenants, cottars and grassmen dependent for at least part of their livelihood on bye-employment — the eventual trebling, even quadrupling of the price of their basic food-stuff was disastrous. Many were unable to grow enough food to feed themselves and not all landowners were prepared to waive or even reduce rents as was Aberdeen's town council. In December 1697 it was reported that some of the town's farms were 'run out and much wasted because of the weakness of the present tenants'. The Dean of Guild was instructed to 'grant defalcation and ease to them for the present crop'.[27] Further up the social scale, John Thomson, wadsetter of Hairmoss in the parish of Monquhitter (who in the Poll Book is recorded as living in the town of Turriff with his wife, son and two servants) was found dead near the coast with raw flesh in his mouth.[28] Among those receiving poor relief in Old Machar were a schoolmaster, a merchant and the widow of an Alford laird.[29]

In Aberdeen three-quarters of those receiving relief in the two lists mentioned previously were women. One of the lists gives the occupation of recipients; two-thirds of the women were widows and the remainder included two old servants and a schoolmistress while seven of the twenty-seven men were tradesmen, one a schoolmaster and another a merchant. Andrew Kerr's 'meaner sort' in 1696 probably consisted of those who were unfree — labourers, porters, sailors, fishermen in the adjacent community of Futtie (who were a particular source of worry to the town council), as well as spinsters and widows — but in November of that year it was claimed that 300 brewers had been ruined because of the high price of malt.[30] There are also several cases of tradesmen unable to feed their apprentices, while John Wright, tacksman of the meal mart, claimed in 1699 that he was having difficulty buying food and pleaded that he and his family should not be reduced to begging because of the hard times.[31] The wealthier Aberdeen merchants and tradesmen, together with anyone who had grain to sell or who was paid in grain, were

relatively immune. When Alexander Thomson, minister of Peterculter, was deposed in 1703 one of the numerous charges against
him was that he had 'got good prices for his victuals in the late
years of dearth, yet he utterly neglected to provide himself with
a competent library'.[32]

As the famine grew worse, many left their parishes to find
food either by begging or theft. In neighbouring Kincardineshire in 1698 and 1699 a number of Aberdeenshire men and
women, mainly from Highland parishes, were convicted of
stealing food. One was a boy from New Deer whose parents had
both died and who had been put up by a Garvock weaver to
steal meal from the mill of Conveth. He was merely expelled
from Kincardineshire but the others were scourged and in some
cases branded. The Stonehaven scourger himself was banished
on suspicion of murdering a man from the Aberdeenshire parish
of Towie.[33]

As the crisis grew worse, increasing numbers of strangers
were buried, some of them in communal graves. The kirk
session register of Kinkell reported that many strangers were
dying there 'in these days of dearth', while twelve strangers
were buried in New Deer during the first ten months of 1698.
At Aberdour in the following year William White received a
shilling for each of the fifteen strangers he had buried.[34] In
Aberdeen some were buried in the links, and in the nearby parish
of Drumoak in April, 1699, the elders complained 'that a gener-
alite of the people . . . were become so unchristian and inhuman
as would not so much help to the churchyard with the dead
bodies of the poor persons who were daily dying before them'.[35]

Such evidence makes it clear that Aberdeenshire suffered
very badly indeed, particularly those areas away from the coast.
But how badly? The answer lies not in contemporary and late
eighteenth century accounts but in the parish registers, un-
promising as they may seem at first sight.[36] Only five of the
eighty-seven parishes at that time have burial registers for at
least part of the crisis. That for Longside, however, is useless because it largely excludes children, who normally made up half
of burials, while those for Methlick and New Deer, although
much more valuable, peter out before the climax of the famine.
The entries for Aberdeen are in the town's Kirk and Bridge
Work Accounts and are of burials in St Nicholas Churchyard
only, although it is clear that fairly substantial numbers of dead
were being buried elsewhere (possible sites are Futtie Churchyard and the former Carmelite Friary as well as the links). The
most reliable one is probably that for Old Machar though here,

# ACT

## For POLE-MONEY.

### June 27. 1695.

THe Eftates of Parliament, taking to their confideration, that in regard of the great and eminent Dangers that threaten this Kingdom from forraign Enemies, and inteftine Difaffection, and the Defigns of Evill Men, and that our Coafts are not fufficiently Secure againft Pria vateers ; and that therefore it is Neceffar, that a compleat Number of Standing Forces be maintained, and Ships of War provided for its neceffary Defence ; as alfo confidering, that befide the Supplie upon the Land-Rent, other Fonds will be requifit for the forefaid End, do for one of thefe Fonds freely and chearfully offer to His Majefty an Subfidy to be uplifted by way of Polemoney, and for making of which Offer Effectuall, His Majefty, with Advice and Confent of the Eftates of Parliament forefaid, doth Statute and Ordain, that all Perfons of whatfoever Age, Sex, or Quality, fhall be fubject and lyable to a Pole of Six Shilling, except Poor Perfons who live upon Charity, and the Children under the Age of Sixteen years, and in familia of all thefe Perfons whofe Pole doth not exceed One Pound Ten Shilling Scots. That befide the faid Six Shilling impofed upon all the Perfons that are not excepted : A Cottar having a Trade fhall pay Six Shilling more, making in the hail Twelve Shilling for every fuch Cottar.

That for Each Servant fhall be payed by the Mafter, for which the Mafter is impowered to retain the fourtieth Part of his yearly Fee, whereof Bounrieth to be reckoned a part ( excepting Livery Cloaths ) in the Number of which Servants are underftood, all who receive Wages or Bounrieth for any Work, or Imployment whatfoever, for the Term or the Year as they have, or fhall ferve, and in Cafe they be not Alimented in Familia with their Mafters, then if they be not above the Degree of a Cottar or Hynd, they are to have two third Parts of Wages and Bountieths, or if above the faid Degree one Third part of Wages and Bountieth, firft deducted for their Aliment.

That all Seamen pay Twelve Shilling Scots in name of Pole.

That all Tennents pay in name of Pole to the King, the hundreth part of the valued Rent, payable by them to the Mafter of the Land, and appoints the Mafter of the Ground to adjuft the Proportions of this Pole amongft his Tennents, according to the refpective Duties payable by them in Money or Victual, efferiring to his valued Rent.

That all Merchants, whether Seamen, Shop-keepers, Chapmen, Tradefmen and others, whofe free Stock and Means ( not including Work-mens Tools, Houfhold-plenifhing; nor Stocks of Tennents upon the Farms and Pofleffion ) is above five hundred Merks, and doth not extend to five thoufand

A         Merks,

Act for pole money, 1695. The act led to the creation of one of the most important sources for the social and economic history of the period, the *List of pollable persons in Aberdeenshire*.

## ABERDEEN the 24 of January 1698.

### ORDERS and INSTRUCTIONS,

For the *Constables* of the Burgh of *Aberdeen*, Made and appointed
be the Magiſtrats, Iuſtices of Peace of the ſaids Burgh, to
be obſerved and gone about by the ſaid *Conſtables*.

### I.

LL the ſaids *Conſtables* or any of them as they ſhall be required, ſhall give
their appearance, when and where the ſaids Magiſtrats ſhall appoint, for
giving Information of any breach of the Peace or other Miſdemeanners; and
receiving Orders and Directions as the ſaids Magiſtrats ſhall enjoyn.

II. Every *Conſtable* in their reſpective Diviſions, ſhall apprehend all Suſ-
pect Perſons, who are Night-walkers, and cannot give a good accompt
of themſelves, and bring them to the Magiſtrats to be taken Order with
as accords: As likewayes all *Vagabonds*, *Idle Sturdie Beggars* and *Extraneans*: As alſo, all
Idle Perſons, who have no Means to live upon, and will not betake themſelves to ſome
Trade.

III. They ſhall apprehend any Guilty of *Slaughter*, *Mother*, *Thiſt*, or any other Capital Crime, and ſhall require the aſſiſtance of their Neighbours for bringing them to the
Magiſtrats.

IV. They ſhall require the aſſiſtance of their Neighbours for ſetling of any Fray or Stirr
betwixt Parties, and if any Parties ſhall flee to an Houſe, The *Conſtable* ſhall follow to the
Houſe, and if the Door be ſhut, he ſhall require the Maſter and Keeper to make open
Doors, which if he refuſe to doe, the *Conſtable* ſhall take Witnes thereupon; and he may
follow in an freſh perſute, although the Partie flee without the bounds of his Charge,
whereupon the *Conſtable* ſhall diſire Concurrence.

V. They are to take up an exact Roll of all the Perſons Inhabitants within their ſeveral
Precincts, *Male* and *Female* above ten years of Age.

VI. They are to require all new *Incomers* to preſent their *Teſtimonials* to one of the
Magiſtrats, that an Note of the ſamen may be taken in the Regiſter for *Teſtimonials*; And
they ſhall delate all ſuch as want *Teſtimonials*, or thoſe that ſets Houſes to Strangers without acquainting the Magiſtrats, or ſuch as ſee Servants without *Teſtimonials*.

VII. They are to delate all *Hotſee-Brewers* within their Precincts.

VIII. They are to delate all Perſons that are to ſind, taking the *Name of God in vain*,
or any otherwayes Swearing or Curſing, eſpecially on the open Streets, or upon *Moca-dayes*:
As likewayes, all *Pykers*, and thoſe under an ill Report or Scandalous.

IX. They ſhall delate all *Inomcators* and *Whoremongers* that comes to their Knowledge.

X. They ſhall delate all *Drunkards* and ſuch as haunt *Taverns* after *Nine aclock at Night*,
and ſuch as ſell Drink in forbidden times, or till Men be Drunk in their Houſes, or
ſuch as ſell Drink above the rate of the Towns Statutes.

XI. They ſhall delate all *Sabbath-Breakers*, and ſuch as wait not upon the Purplick Ordi-
nances of GODS Worſhip, or breakes the *Lords Day* any other manner of way: And for
this end, Two or Three of them are to go thorow the Town (*Per Vices*) in time of fore
and *Afternoons Sermons*, to obſerve what Order is kept in the Town upon the *Lords Day*.

XII. They are to delate all *Scolds*, *Tulzers*, and ſuch as make Plyes.

XIII. They are to delate Children come to years of Diſcretion that are Diſobedient
to their Parents, or Servants Diſobedient to their Maſters: As alſo, ſuch Servants as ſhall
be found *Stealers* and *Pykers* of their Maſters Goods or Houſhold Plenſhing.

XIV. They ſhall delate ſuch as tranſgreſs any of the Statutes publiſhed by the Magiſtrats that they may be Puniſhed.

XV. They ſhall have Four General Meetings in the Year, (*viz.*) one at the beginning of each Quarter, for conſidering all the Affairs paſt in the preceeding Quarter.

XVI. They ſhall meet each *Monday* at *Nine-aclock* in the *Morning*, in the *Laugh-
Councill Houſe*, for keeping their Weekly Courts, and Ilk Abſent to be fined in *Twelve ſhil-
ling ſcots* (*Toties quoties*.) And if any *Conſtable* ſhall be found negligent of his Duty, to be
Cenſured as the Magiſtrats ſhall think fit.

Extracted forth of the Iuſtice Court Books of *Aberdeen*, by
*Maſter Alexander Thomſon Town Clerk* of the ſaid Burgh.

### AL: THOMSON, Cls.

Orders for the constables of Aberdeen, 1698, issued by the magistrates of the burgh acting as justices of the peace.

too, some dead were buried in places other than the parish churchyard. Moreover, at the height of the crisis the Commissioners of Supply for Aberdeenshire ordered that the poor should be buried where they fell.[37]

There are five usable marriage registers though only that for Old Machar has entries for every year between 1690 and 1705, and three of the remainder, somewhat surprisingly, begin during the crisis. Baptismal registers are much more plentiful though some of those that have survived (Auchindoir, Huntly, Leochel, New Machar and Strichen) are too fragmentary to be of use and many of the remaining twenty have gaps, particularly at the height of the famine when a number of sesssion-clerks died. They are also unevenly distributed (see Figure 1). The Aberdeen area and Buchan are fairly well represented, but the heavily populated Garioch has only registers for Keith-hall and Kemnay — neither very good — and the Highland area only for Strathdon, whose register is practically illegible. Nevertheless, they are an extremely valuable source.

When using parish registers, 'harvest years' give a better indication of the impact of famine on burials, baptisms and marriages than calendar years. Such 'harvest years' begin in October: thus the harvest year 1695 lies mainly in the calendar year 1696, running from October 1695 to September 1696. Moreover, figures for quarters and even single months make it possible to examine the course of the crisis in detail and even to suggest possible causes of death.

Dealing with the handful of burial registers first, all four show no significant increase in mortality during the harvest year 1695 despite the bad harvest and subsequent doubling of prices; indeed, in Aberdeen and Old Machar burials were actually below the annual average for 1690-4 (see Table 2). The following harvest year, however, saw a massive increase in burials, particularly free ones, in Aberdeen, Old Machar and New Deer; the increase in Methlick was much less marked. In the third year of the crisis they fell sharply in Aberdeen, remained about the same in Old Machar, and rose dramatically in Methlick and New Deer — in the last they were four times higher than the pre-famine level even though the worst year was yet to come. This was the harvest year 1698 when 377 were buried in St Nicholas Churchyard (244 of them free) and 242 in Old Machar, about twice as many as the average from 1690-4. Unfortunately, the registers for Methlick and New Deer effectively end before the completion of the year, although that for New Deer contains some entries of multiple burials of members of the same family

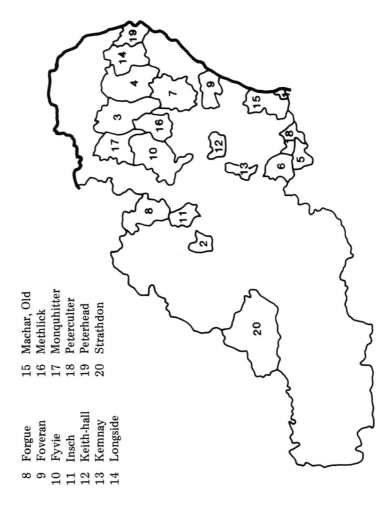

1  Aberdeen
2  Clatt
3  Deer, New
4  Deer, Old
5  Drumoak
6  Echt
7  Ellon

8   Forgue
9   Foveran
10  Fyvie
11  Insch
12  Keith-hall
13  Kemnay
14  Longside

15  Machar, Old
16  Methlick
17  Monquhitter
18  Peterculter
19  Peterhead
20  Strathdon

Figure 1   Aberdeenshire: parishes with baptismal registers, c. 1690-1705

and below the final entry in June 1700, is written 'Thar is Above Sax Scor of poor' which may refer to free burials after October 1698 when a new session clerk stopped including them. Even without these, however, it is clear that the level of mortality in New Deer and, to a lesser extent, Methlick was considerably higher than in Aberdeen and Old Machar.

TABLE 2

*Burials in four Aberdeenshire parishes (free burials in brackets): harvest years (October-September), 1690-1704*

| Harvest year | Aberdeen | Old Machar | Methlick | New Deer |
|---|---|---|---|---|
| 1690-4(av.) | 178.4(55.6) | 125.4 | 44.3(3) | 41.3[3] |
| 1695 | 154 (44) | 94 | 50 (7) | 42 (4) |
| 1696 | 349(169) | 182 | 54(10) | 98(33) |
| 1697 | 231(107) | 178 | 92(40) | 163(40) |
| 1698 | 377(244) | 242 | 77(46)[2] | |
| 1699 | 130 (46) | 52 | | |
| 1700-4(av.) | 113.8(22.8)[1] | 76.2 | | |

1  1700-3 only       2  October-June only
3  average of 1691, 1694 and 1695 only

In the last two the fall in burials came quite suddenly in October 1699 and, although two children died on the streets in Aberdeen during that month and 'a poor stranger man' in September 1700, it was particularly marked in the case of free burials. Burials in Aberdeen in 1699-1703 were fewer than two-thirds of those in the five years before the famine (see Figure 2), and in Old Machar the fall was even greater. The famine had removed the weakest, many of them prematurely; the result was a healthier population with a much lower proportion of the old and the poor than before and therefore a lower death rate.

The Aberdeen and Methlick registers indicate burials of infants and children which did not rise at all during the crisis. In part this can be explained, as we shall see, by a reduction in the numbers of babies born and therefore in infant mortality but it may well be that infants and children had a greater resistance to starvation and some of the diseases, notably typhus, associated with it.

In Old Machar the peak of mortality occurred in the second quarter of 1699 (April, May, June) when death from shortage

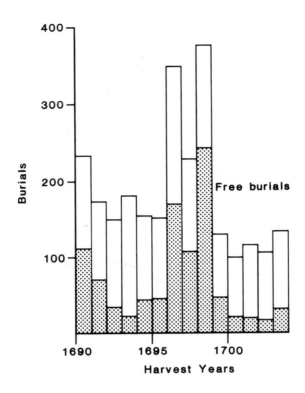

Figure 2    Burials in St Nicholas' Churchyard, Aberdeen,
harvest years 1690-1703

of food was most likely, but there was hardly a month for three
years when mortality was not considerably higher than before
the famine. In Aberdeen free burials also reached their peak
then, but total burials were actually at their highest in the last
quarter of 1698 when food would be more plentiful. This, together with the relatively low infant and child mortality, suggests
that death from starvation (e.g. famine dropsy) was not the
only or even the main cause of high mortality. Contemporary
accounts frequently refer to 'fevers' which are most likely
typhus, a disease which has always been associated with famine.[38] Conditions in Aberdeenshire were probably very similar
to those in Ireland during the Great Famine where, to quote
one medical historian:

The lack of cleanliness, the unchanged clothing and crowding together, provided conditions ideal for lice to multiply and spread
rapidly ... In such circumstances an initial case or two of fever
could serve to infect a whole district. In general the worse the
famine in any part, the more intense the fever, and crowds of
starving people forsook their homes and took to the road, thus
carrying disease with them wherever they went.[39]

Another frequently famine-related disease mentioned by
contemporaries was the 'flux' or dysentry which was probably
caused by eating rotten food and, like typhus, was spread by
beggars. Other diseases such as measles and influenza were undoubtedly made much deadlier as a result of malnutrition while
pneumonia was probably caused by a combination of hunger,
bad weather and a shortage of peat fuel.[40]

The small number of burial registers and the fact that at the
climax of the crisis they underestimate the extent of mortality
means that any attempt to measure the severity of the famine
and its regional distribution must be based on the more numerous baptismal registers. Baptisms, in fact, are much more
sensitive to a rise in prices than burials, at least in the beginning of a crisis.

TABLE 3

*Conceptions in seven Aberdeenshire parishes:[1] harvest years*
*(October-September), 1690-1704*

| Parish | 1690-4 | 1695 | 1696 | 1697 | 1698 | 1699 | 1700-4 |
|---|---|---|---|---|---|---|---|
| Number of conceptions | 617 | 448 | 393 | 382 | 316 | 501 | 524.4 |
| Index | 100.0 | 72.6 | 63.7 | 61.9 | 51.2 | 81.2 | 85.2 |

1   Aberdeen, Echt, Forgue, Fyvie, Insch, Methlick,
Old Deer and Old Machar

In the seven registers that provide figures for every month
of the harvest years 1690-1704, conceptions (i.e. baptisms less
nine months) started to fall as early as the winter of 1696,
particularly in Aberdeen, Old Machar and Old Deer, and continued to decline until the end of the crisis (see Table 3). By
1698 conceptions in the seven parishes were only half of what
they had been between 1690 and 1694. The decline, however,

was not equal since it tended to worsen away from the Aberdeen area and along the coast; conceptions in Aberdeen, Old Machar, Echt and Peterhead were over fifty-five per cent of 1690-4 while in Methlick, Fyvie, Forgue and Strathdon they ranged between thirty and forty per cent (see Table 4).

TABLE 4

*Conceptions in 1698 (harvest year)*
*as a percentage of 1690-4 (average)*

| Over 50 per cent | | 40-49 per cent | | 30-39 per cent | |
|---|---|---|---|---|---|
| 1 Aberdeen | 64.7 | 5 Old Deer | 47.2 | 8 Methlick | 38.8 |
| 2 Old Machar | 57.2 | 6 Insch | 44.9 | 9 Fyvie | 34.4 |
| 3 Echt | 55.6 | 7 Longside | 42.5 | 10 Forgue | 31.0 |
| 4 Peterhead | 55.3 | | | 11 Strathdon | 30.6 |

In part the reduction was the result of a fall in marriages, which in Old Machar began as early as the autumn of 1695, but this was much less marked than for conceptions. The most obvious explanation is a combination of lessened sexual activity, loss of marriage partners, an increase in spontaneous abortions, and famine amenorrhea (a temporary loss of fertility in women). This was probably the case in the three years of high mortality, particularly in the harvest year 1698, but as we have seen, mortality in the harvest year 1695 did not rise and yet conceptions fell by about a quarter. The same phenomenon has been noted in famines elsewhere and suggests that there may have been family limitation (e.g. sexual abstinence, deliberate abortions and coitus interruptus) in anticipation of difficult times ahead.[41]

The fall in population in Aberdeenshire, therefore, was caused by an increase in mortality over three years, a fall in births over four years (which reduced replacement levels) and, much less easy to quantify, large numbers of people leaving Aberdeenshire in search of food. Professor Smout has suggested that for Scotland as a whole the fall in births and emigration together may have accounted for half the decline in population, leaving the increase in mortality responsible for the other half.[42]

The twenty baptismal registers provide figures for most of the calendar years 1691-5 and 1701-5. When Aberdeenshire is divided into four regions (see Figure 3), they show that in Aberdeen itself, baptisms were nearly thirteen per cent lower in 1701-5 than in 1691-5, in the sample of six parishes in the area

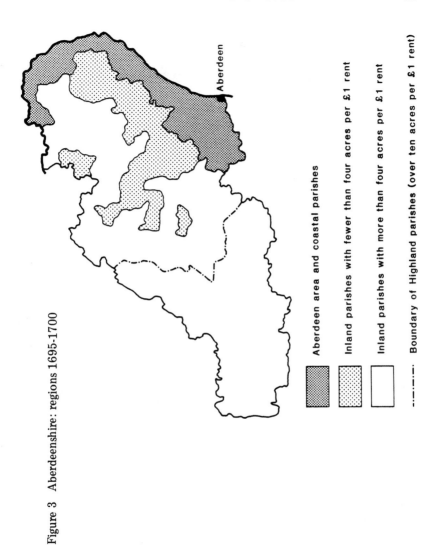

Figure 3   Aberdeenshire: regions 1695-1700

Aberdeen

Aberdeen area and coastal parishes

Inland parishes with fewer than four acres per £1 rent

Inland parishes with more than four acres per £1 rent

Boundary of Highland parishes (over ten acres per £1 rent)

around Aberdeen and along the coast three per cent lower, in
the seven inland parishes of the sample with fewer than four
acres per £1 rent twenty-one per cent lower, and in the six
parishes in the less fertile parts of Aberdeenshire, including the
Highlands, whose registers have survived, twenty-six per cent
lower (see Table 5).

TABLE 5

*Baptisms per annum c. 1691-5 and 1706-10*

| Region | No. of parishes in sample | No. of baptisms | | |
| --- | --- | --- | --- | --- |
| | | *c.*1691-5 | *c.*1701-5 | *c.*1706-10 |
| | | (Index: *c.*1691-5 = 100.0) | | |
| 1  Aberdeen | 1 | 190.6 (100.0) | 166.6 (87.4) | 166.8 (87.5) |
| 2  Aberdeen area and coastal parishes | 6 | 310.4 (100.0) | 300.4 (96.8) | 315.0 (101.5) |
| 3  Inland parishes with fewer than 4 acres per £ rent of 1674 | 7 | 319.5 (100.0) | 253.1 (79.2) | — — |
| [3  excluding Clatt | 6 | 292.1 (100.0) | 231.1 (79.1) | 259.2 ] (88.7)] |
| 4  Inland parishes with more than 4 acres per £ rent of 1674 | 6 | 380.3 (100.0) | 280.7 (73.8) | — — |
| [4  excluding Strathdon | 5 | 295.9 (100.0) | 222.7 (75.3) | 266.2 ] (90.0)] |

    Mortality crises were generally followed by an upsurge in
marriages of couples who had been unable to marry during the
crisis, of widows and widowers re-marrying, and of couples
marrying earlier than they might otherwise have done because
of vacancies in jobs and tenancies left by those who had died,
which in turn would lead to an increase in births. Moreover,
because of the deaths of so many old people, the average age of
the surviving population was lower. The result, therefore, was a
higher birthrate that before the crisis.[43] This was probably the
case in and around Aberdeen and along the coast, which would
mean that their fall in population was greater than that in births.

If we assume that the crude birth rate rose from thirty per 1,000 in 1691-5 to thirty-three per 1,000 in 1701-5,[44] the population of Aberdeen fell by twenty per cent and that of the other region by twelve per cent (see Table 6). The disparity between the two can be explained by the fact that Aberdeen normally had a surplus of deaths over births and needed to attract immigrants to grow or merely prevent a decline; during the famine, however, not only did immigration cease but many left the town, voluntarily or otherwise. In the remaining two regions, however, it could be argued that the famine was so severe and caused such indebtedness and poverty that there was no rise in the birth rate, at least until after 1705, and that the fall in population there was the same as the reduction in births. The eighteenth century Swiss pioneer of demographic and socio-economic statistics, Johann Heinrich Waser, discussed this problem and concluded:

> ... the crisis caused by pestilence can be compensated within a decade. Damages brought by famine and starvation, however, have more severe consequences, because after these catastrophes

TABLE 6

*Population of Aberdeenshire, 1695-1801*

| Region | No. of parishes | 1695 (estimate) | 1700 (estimate) | 1755 | 1801 |
|---|---|---|---|---|---|
| 1 Aberdeen | 1 | 7,142 | 5,674[1] | 10,785 | 17,597 |
| 2 Aberdeen area and coastal parishes | 22 | 33,134 | 29,155[1] | 30,719 | 37,134 |
| 3 Inland parishes with fewer than 4 acres per £ rent of 1674 | 22 | 28,259 | 22,381[2] | 25,422 | 23,372 |
| 4 Inland parishes with more than 4 acres per £1 rent of 1674 | 41 | 55,712 | 41,115[2] | 49,174 | 43,888 |
| Total | 86 | 124,247 | 98,325 | 116,100 | 121,991 |

1   Assuming crude birth rate rose from 30 per 1,000 in 1691-5 to 33 per 1,000 in 1701-5
2   Assuming crude birth rate was 30 per 1,000 in both 1691-5 and 1701-5

TABLE 7

*Increase or decrease in population of Aberdeenshire, 1695-1801*

| Region | 1695-1700 | 1700-55 | 1755-1801 |
|---|---|---|---|
| 1  Aberdeen | −20.6 | +90.1 | +63.2 |
| 2  Aberdeen area and coastal parishes | −12.0 | + 5.4 | +20.9 |
| 3  Inland parishes with fewer than 4 acres per £ rent of 1674 | −20.8 | +13.6 | − 8.1 |
| 4  Inland parishes with more than 4 acres per £1 rent of 1674 | −26.2 | +19.6 | −10.7 |
| Total | −20.9 | +18.1 | + 5.1 |

the impoverished, worn-out and discouraged people are in want of the dearest [*sic.*] necessities of life and will need years to recover. Whoever is not in the highest degree careless will think twice before he gets married, and due to the fact that children will not be considered a blessing of God but rather a burden of married life, the population will increase very slowly.[45]

Using the method of calculating the population of Aberdeenshire in 1695 described in a recent article in *Northern Scotland*[46] and assuming that the twenty parish registers provide a reasonable sample, the four regions had a combined population at that date of 124,000, which fell to 98,000 by the end of the crisis. This is a decline of no less than twenty-one per cent which was not made good by the time of Webster's census in 1755 (see Table 7). Such an estimate is based upon too many assumptions to be more than speculative but given the intensity of the famine, particularly in the interior of Aberdeenshire, and the fact that it was spread over four years, it is by no means improbable. In Finland, for example, upward of a third of the population may have died in the single year of 1697.[47]

## REFERENCES

1   E.A. Wrigley and R.S. Schofield, *The population history of England, 1541-1871* (London, 1981), 341.

2   M.W. Flinn (ed.), *Scottish population history from the seventeenth century to the 1930s* (Cambridge, 1977), 164-86.

3   Sir John Sinclair (ed.), *[First] statistical account of Scotland [FSA]* (21 vols., 1791-9), vi, 132.

4   J. Anderson, *General view of the agriculture of the county of Aberdeen* (Edinburgh, 1794), 175-7.

5   H.H. Lamb, 'The Little Ice Age period and the great storms within it', in M.J. Tooley and G.M. Sheail (eds.), *The climatic scene* (London, 1985), 107-110.

6   M.L. Parry, *Climatic change, agriculture and settlement* (Folkstone, 1978), 73-82.

7   J. Stuart (ed.), *List of pollable persons within the shire of Aberdeen, 1696* (2 vols., Aberdeen, 1844). The lists for each parish were compiled in September 1695.

8   'An account of Buchan and what is remarkable therein' in J. Robertson (ed.), *Collections for the history of the shires of Aberdeen and Banff* (Spalding Club, 1843), i, 96.

9   T.C. Smout, *Scottish trade on the eve of the Union, 1660-1707* (Edinburgh, 1963), 142, 235.

10   W. Kennedy, *Annals of Aberdeen* (2 vols., Aberdeen, 1818), i, 248.

11   H. Scott (ed.), *Fasti ecclesiae Scoticanae, vi, Synods of Aberdeen and Moray* (new ed., Edinburgh, 1926).

12   Old Machar Kirk Session Accounts, 1675-1698 and 1698-1720, G.D. Henderson and H.H. Porter (eds.), *James Gordon's diary 1692-1710* (Third Spalding Club, 1949), 81.

13   Old Machar Kirk Session Accounts, *passim*.

14   Aberdeen District Archives [ADA], Town Council Register, lvii, 534. I would like to thank Miss Judith Cripps, Aberdeen City Archivist, for her assistance with this and other sources.

15   ADA, Town Council Register, lvii, 556; Scottish Record Office [SRO], CH. 2/448/23, Aberdeen Kirk Session Register, 1694-7, 184.

16   ADA, Aberdeen Council Letter Book, vii, no. 243.

17   SRO, CH. 2/448/24.

18   ADA, Aberdeen Justice Court, Accounts, 1657-1744, *passim*.

19   ADA, Aberdeen Kirk and Bridge Work Accounts, i and ii, *passim*.

20   ADA, Town Council Register, lvii, 642-3.

21   Ibid., lvii, 652.

22   Ibid., lvii, 534.

23   Ibid., lvii, 622, 645, 647, 652, 686. An Aberdeen peck of meal was

just over 8lbs. 11oz.

24    Ibid., lvii, 693.

25    *FSA*, vi, 132; I. Whyte, *Agriculture and society in seventeenth century Scotland* (Edinburgh, 1979), 248.

26    *Acts of the parliament of Scotland*, xi, (1824), 166.

27    ADA, Town Council Register, vii, 620.

28    *FSA*, vi, 132.

29    Old Machar Kirk Session Accounts, *passim*.

30    ADA, Town Council Register, vii, 544.

31    SRO, CH. 2/448/23, Aberdeen Kirk Session Register, 184; ADA, Town Council Register, lvii, 693.

32    J.A. Henderson, *Annals of Lower Deeside* (Aberdeen, 1892), 140.

33    J. Anderson, *The black book of Kincardineshire* (Stonehaven, 1843), 62-81.

34    Flinn, *Scottish population history*, 168; J. McPherson, 'The famine years in the North East', *Transactions of the Banffshire Field Club* (1933), 51.

35    Henderson, *Annals of Lower Deeside*, 102.

36    Most Aberdeenshire parish registers are held in the General Register Office, New Register House, Edinburgh, but microfilm copies are available in Aberdeen Central Library.

37    Flinn, *Scottish population history*, 170.

38    A.B. Appleby, *Famine in Tudor and Stuart England* (Liverpool, 1978), 102-3.

39    W.P. MacArthur, 'Medical history of the famine', in R.D. Edwards and T.D. Williams (eds.), *The Great Famine* (Dublin, 1956), 271-2.

40    Ibid., 265-89.

41    Wrigley and Schofield, *The population history of England*, 359-73; E. Le Roy Ladurie, 'Famine amenorrhoea' in R. Forster and O. Ranum (eds.), *Biology of man in history* (Baltimore and London, 1975), 163-78; H. Charbonneau and A. Larose (eds.), *The great mortalities: methodological studies of demographic crisis in the past* (Liege, 1980?), 317-18.

42    Flinn, *Scottish population history*, 181.

43    Wrigley and Schofield, *The population history of England*, 359-63.

44    R.E. Tyson, 'The population of Aberdeenshire, 1695-1755: a new approach', *Northern Scotland*, vi, no. 1 (1985), 126.

45    Quoted by R. Braun, 'Early industrialization and demographic change in the canton of Zurich' in C. Tilly (ed.), *Historical studies of changing fertility* (Princeton, 1978), 324.

46    Tyson, 'The population of Aberdeenshire', 113-31.

47    E. Jutikkala, 'The great Finnish famine in 1696-97', *Scandinavian Economic History Review*, iii, no. 1 (1955), 48-63.

# THE EVOLUTION OF SETTLEMENT IN BUCHAN SINCE THE LATE SIXTEENTH CENTURY: THE EVIDENCE FROM CARTOGRAPHIC SOURCES AND FROM THE 1696 POLL TAX ASSESSMENT

## JAMES R. COULL

As the full text of this paper has been published elsewhere only a summary is printed here.[1]

A series of five maps are available for the Buchan district: those of Timothy Pont (*c.* 1590); James and Robert Gordon (*c.* 1640); General William Roy (*c.* 1750); John Thomson (1826); and the original Ordnance Survey (1876). Along with the material in the Aberdeenshire Poll Book (1696),[2] these allow a study of settlement evolution over the period 1590-1876. This shows the build-up of rural settlement to its all-time peak, as from the late nineteenth century there was a thinning out, with accelerated migration into the towns.

All the sources have limitations as to their completeness and their accuracy; but in general the standard of recording and of cartography improved with time. While it cannot be doubted that there was a proliferation of settlement over the period, it is rarely possible to demonstrate this in detail. Spellings of individual names vary considerably in the maps, and on occasions show either distinctive Scottish spelling conventions or the influence of local dialect; but this virtually never causes problems of identification. In a number of cases, however, places are inadequately specified. The biggest issues here are places categorised as 'mains' or 'mill' without a qualifying element: such placenames are so frequent that on the map-scales employed definite identification is often impossible.

Problems of identification also arise with places which cannot be located on modern maps. This can arise either through the names of places being changed or their being abandoned: definite cases are known of both, but in most cases the fate of places which do not occur on modern maps cannot be ascertained.

The greatest problems of identification arise on the later maps, which show large numbers of places without naming them: it is impossible to identify with certainty most of these un-named places on the Roy and Thomson maps, although those on the First Ordnance Survey can be checked against valuation rolls.

In a number of cases it is clear that the Thomson and First Ordnance Survey maps generalise by designating a number of settlements with a single collective name. While it is not impossible that some of the names on earlier maps have a collective sense, each name is regularly associated with only a single symbol.

While the later maps are generally more accurate, it is relatively easy to recognise numbers of errors on all maps apart from the First Ordnance Survey. These occur mainly in the erroneous positioning of some places vis-a-vis their neighbours, but mis-spellings and other errors may occasionally be identified. Also the comparison of the maps with each other and with other documents show that all apart from the First Ordnance Survey omit places known to have been in existence at the time that they were made.

Despite the limitations of the sources, however, they do demonstrate strong elements of continuity in the settlement pattern as well as considerable expansion. The places consistently recorded on all sources are biased towards the more important ones — especially towns, parish centres and leading estate houses. However, complete continuity in all sources can be demonstrated for only 139 settlements, out of a total of 425 on the Pont map.

The sources indicate a continuous and accelerating increase in the number of settlements with time, from a total of 425 in the Pont map to 2,554 on the First Ordnance Survey: this apparent six-fold increase must however be an exaggeration due to improving cartography. The distribution of settlement at all times reflected the basic factors of physical geography, with concentration on the best land for farming, and settlement thinner or absent on the poorer land, which included sandy coastal stretches, peat mosses, and hilly and broken terrain. Over time settlement intensified on the best land, and there was some movement of the frontiers of cultivation at the edges of the poorer land.

The familiar process of township splitting in the evolution of Scottish settlement is shown on the maps, but seldom as a complete or dependable sequence. Already at the time of Pont there were over 30 cases of multiple townships sharing the same basic name (e.g. East and West Birness); and although recording is irregular on the different maps, it is clear by the First Ordnance Survey that splitting had occurred in many cases and had often gone through several phases: in the case of places like Hythie and Knaven up to five places shared the same basic name. In addition to township splitting there had been considerable settlement over the period at the edges of cultivation, shown by a range of names like Moss-side and Boghead.

There is controversy in Scotland as to how much change there was during the improving movement, which in this area was mainly concentrated between *c.* 1780 and *c.* 1810. The Roy map of *c.* 1750 shows a pattern dominated by 'ferm toun' clusters of from four to seven buildings, and the single symbols of the Thomson map of 1826 suggests a complete transition to single farms; but this transition is likely to be exaggerated by the stylised symbols adopted in both cases.

The seven burghs of the district were regularly recorded apart from the omission of Rosehearty by Roy. The later sources demonstrate the way in which the burghs were growing, and by the time of the First Ordnance Survey there is also some evident growth in old parish centres like Crimond and Old Deer. Over time there is also the development of sixteen bigger settlements in the coastal fishing villages, while the twelve inland planned villages from the improving era are prominently recorded on the Thomson map; and the First Ordnance Survey shows the impact of the recently arrived railway with the junction of Maud and stations like Auchnagatt.

Of the settlements which vanish from the record over time, which total well over a hundred, it is generally not possible to give a definite reason for disappearance. A few changes of name are known (e.g. Altrie became Bruxie, and Rotnachy became Craigellie); at the coast Forvie was over-blown with sand, while Rattray was cut off from the sea by the accumulation of a bay-bar. Another possible reason in some cases must be the impact of periodic dearth and epidemics, especially in the period before 1700.

To conclude, the comparative study of the map cover is the best available means for showing the evolution of settlement at the district level in this part of Scotland; but a fuller understanding of the process would include other documents, especially estate papers.

## REFERENCES

1    J.R. Coull, *The evolution of settlement in the Buchan district of Aberdeenshire* (O'Dell Memorial Monograph no. 17, Department of Geography, University of Aberdeen, 1984).

2    J. Stuart (ed.), *List of pollable persons within the shire of Aberdeen, 1696* (2 vols., Aberdeen, 1844).

Town Councillors.
  17 merchant burgesss
   2 craftman

350 merchant gild members.
of these about 300 were active traders.
but only about 75 in any one year
traded - musels.

# MERCHANTS AND TRADERS IN EARLY
# SEVENTEENTH CENTURY ABERDEEN

## DUNCAN MACNIVEN

The paper[1] considers four main questions about mercantile life in Aberdeen between 1590 and 1640:

What part did merchants and traders play in the life of the town?

How were trade patterns changing in the early seventeenth century?

What scope was there for social mobility? *Very little.*

Did Aberdeen prosper?

## The merchants' part in burgh life

In the early seventeenth century, Aberdeen was Scotland's third town (in terms of the taxation which it paid, exceeded only by Edinburgh and Dundee). It was the cultural, economic, educational, legal and governmental centre of North East Scotland. Despite its importance, it covered a very small area — a couple of hundred yards' radius around the junction of the Castlegate and Broadgate (modern Broad Street). The burgh was the focus of an area in which its burgesses had a monopoly of trade in foreign goods and exported Scottish wares and of all manufactures. This area — the 'liberty' of the burgh — extended in theory throughout the sheriffdom, but in practice the monopoly had been eroded by newer burghs such as Fraserburgh, Peterhead, Turriff and Newburgh.

There is little firm contemporary evidence of the size of Aberdeen's population at the time. It was perhaps between 7,500 and 10,000.[2] Of these, about 350 were members of the merchant gild (twenty to thirty new members being admitted annually). Perhaps around 300 of these gild members were active traders, and only about seventy-five in any one year traded overseas.[3] The merchant gild burgess was not invariably rich: some merchants were among the poorest burgesses and some members of the craft gilds were among the wealthiest. But the merchant gild was powerful and prestigious. It was powerful largely because it dominated the town council. Seventeen of the nineteen councillors were merchant burgesses — drawn, in practice, mostly from only about half a dozen families (the Chambers,

Menzies, Cullen, Collinson, Lawson, Gray, Rutherford and
Leslie families). The remaining two councillors were craftsmen;
but, in order to restrict the power they wielded on the town
council, the craft councillors changed annually. The merchant
gild was prestigious in the sense that it included the most prominent men in the legal, religious and educational (as well as
mercantile) life of the town, together with landowners from the
surrounding countryside.

Aside from their political and social importance, members
of the merchant gild played an important part in the economic
life of the burgh. They had a statutory monopoly of all foreign
trade in the liberty, and of trade in certain staple goods (including fish, hides, wool and cloth) — except that craftsmen could
trade these staples if they consisted of either the raw material
or the finished product of their craft. Craftsmen could also
trade in non-staple goods. But, strictly speaking, people from
outside the burgh were not permitted to trade in goods, other
than by selling their own produce at their local markets or at
the burgh markets.

How did the merchants operate? Firstly, they bought goods
from the liberty — either by buying directly from the country
folk (legally, in local markets, or illegally elsewhere), or from
country folk at the burgh markets, or from other Aberdeen
merchants who acted as middlemen. The main commodities
were plaiding (coarse woollen cloth), hides, wool and live
animals. Secondly, they bought goods produced in Aberdeen,
including manufactured woollen goods, leather and fish. Thirdly,
they traded by sea within Scotland and abroad. They traded to
relatively few locations (partly because Leith and Campvere
acted as entrepots); and individual merchants tended to concentrate (although not exclusively) on one trading centre. And
relatively few commodities were involved — Aberdeen and its
hinterland produced a restricted range of commodities and the
area was neither wealthy enough nor sophisticated enough to
need a wide range of imports. Let us look at the main locations
of the trade, and the commodities associated with each.[4]

Firstly, there was the local coastwise trade. Grain was brought
in from Ross, the Black Isle and Buchan — normally for re-
export. Cattle were imported mainly for the needs of the burgh
(food, and hides for making leather). Much wool came from the
surrounding area — initially mostly for re-export (especially to
Flanders and Danzig) but increasingly wool was manufactured
in the burgh into plaiding, stockings and bonnets for export to
the Baltic, north France and Flanders. Hides were brought in

mainly from Moray and the Mearns and were initially re-exported unprocessed. But in the 1610s and 1620s more and more hides were treated with alum to make leather and, by the 1630s, gloves were being manufactured for export. Fish came into Aberdeen in small quantities from ports all along the coast. They were barrelled and exported — salmon especially to north France, and herring and other whitefish to the Baltic and to France. Lastly, wood and stone were imported for use within the town.

②    Secondly, merchants traded to Dundee and Leith, which both acted as entrepots. Dundee served as an entrepot particularly for Baltic goods but Leith's role was much more extensive. All the commodities exported from Aberdeen were sold there — and, in return, came coal, wool from the Borders and many manufactured imports including dyes and cloths.

③    England was the third area with which Aberdeen traded, though a relatively minor one. Aberdeen's principal export was grain and it imported beer (especially from King's Lynn), cloth (especially from Yorkshire) and Flemish goods (from London).

④    Fourthly, there was much trade with Scandinavia, although few commodities were involved. Most of the trade was with Norway, whence came large quantities of wood of various sorts; little passed in the opposite direction. Sweden was a further source of timber and of iron, while from Denmark came malt for brewing. The Baltic (the towns of the former Hanseatic League) was Aberdeen's second most important trading partner in terms of value. The main centre was Danzig — where there was a thriving community of Aberdonians. To the Baltic was sent the full range of the burgh's exports (particularly plaiding, stockings, leather, herring and grain). In exchange came beer, specialised woods (especially for making barrels), iron, lead, tar, salt and (in times of good harvest in the Baltic) grain.

In the Low Countries there were two centres of trade. Salt was imported from Amsterdam but the main centre of trade (and probably Aberdeen's main trade route, in volume and value) was with Campvere in Zeeland. The town of Campvere was the Scottish staple port in the Low Countries, through which by law all trade was to be channelled. The full range of Aberdeen's exports was sent there (particularly plaiding, raw wool, salmon and grain). Imports consisted of raw materials (hops, lint, hemp, starch, dyes and alum), manufactured goods (such as pipes, pans, fine cloth — and the bells for St Nicholas Church) and foodstuffs (apples, onions, spices and exotic foods).

Finally, the trade with France. There were two main centres

— north France, especially Dieppe (to which the principal export was salmon in large quantities, and from which small quantities of luxury goods including fine textiles were returned to Aberdeen) and the Biscay ports (wine imported from Bordeaux and salt from La Rochelle).

That, then, was the restricted range of Aberdeen's trading contacts. Only occasionally did Aberdeen's merchants trade with other centres such as Spain; and there is record in the period of only one merchant trading to the New World (Virginia).

### Changing trade patterns

Two main sources allow us to quantify commercial trends. The first is the Shore Work Accounts — the record of the receipts from a duty levied on all trade passing through the port of Aberdeen and used for maintaining the harbour.[4] The second source is the Exchequer Rolls — central government records which set out the quantity of certain exported goods and the quantity of wine imported.[5] Neither source is entirely accurate (and, unfortunately, neither is consistent in accuracy), so I have used their information with caution — and tried to buttress it by evidence from non-quantitative sources wherever possible. These two sources (illustrated in Figures 1 and 2) show three successive periods of increasing commerce between 1600 and 1650. There may indeed have been a fourth (in the early 1590s, when circumstantial evidence such as the willingness of burgesses to contribute to the founding of Marischal College suggests particular prosperity) but we cannot be certain, because that period pre-dates both quantitative sources.

The first certain period of growth was between 1605 and 1610. Imports and exports alike increased. Growth in the Norwegian and Flemish trade was only partly counterbalanced by decline in trade with France and the Baltic. The Shore Work Accounts' evidence of expansion is substantiated by the fact that Aberdeen merchants acquired one (possibly two) new ships — and a further ship, appropriately called the Bonacord, was built in Aberdeen, using timber floated down the Dee.

After 1610, the level of trade was maintained, with expansion in some sectors such as the export of salmon and plaiding, until the ensuing period of expansion between 1615 and 1623-4. Imports particularly grew in volume — notably the Baltic trade (in beer and grain). Coastwise trade in grain from Buchan, Ross and Caithness more than doubled between 1617-18 and 1621-2 — a consequence, doubtless, of the extensive famine in much of Scotland in the early 1620s. As a result of this commercial

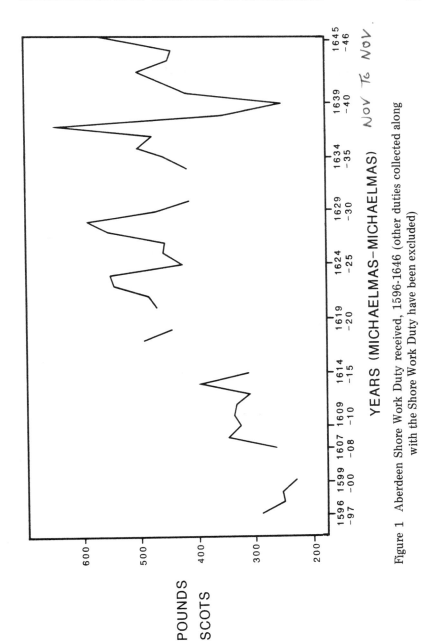

Figure 1 Aberdeen Shore Work Duty received, 1596-1646 (other duties collected along with the Shore Work Duty have been excluded)

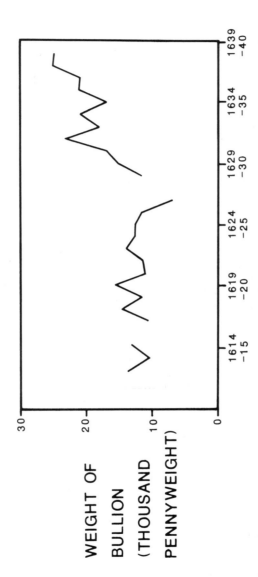

Figure 2  Exchequer Rolls — Bullion Duty received on Aberdeen
exports, 1612-1639

boom the burgh had enough money to undertake several public works — the construction of two mills operated by the tide, the building of a steeple on the tolbooth (which still survives) and the eastward extension of the quay (evidence of which was revealed by excavation in the 1970s) — as well as giving a grant to the marquis of Huntly to build a bridge over the Bogie and a cart road from the Deveron to the Spey. By 1623-4, the Shore Work receipts were roughly double their level nine years previously.

This period of expansion was succeeded by lean years between 1625 and 1627. Trade in grain returned to approximately its pre-famine level. But French trade actually declined, because of the deteriorating political situation which culminated in outright war in April 1627. Two Aberdeen ships were being held in Dunkirk in July 1627. But recovery followed and total trade at the end of the decade was roughly at the same level as in the early 1620s.

The third period of expansion took place from 1630 to 1638. Unlike the previous increases, this was export-based. Not all trade routes prospered. Trade with Norway and the Baltic declined slightly, the home demand for wood, beer and grain having fallen. But the growth points more than compensated. In particular, exports to Flanders (especially plaiding) increased and so did general trade with France, England and the rest of Scotland. As a result, the 1630s saw a further period of public works — the building of a slaughterhouse in 1631, the founding of a craft hospital in 1632, the refurbishment of Greyfriars Church and the provision of a new water supply in 1633 and the establishment of a correction house (where minor offenders wove cloth) in 1636. Most relevant to Aberdeen's merchants was the construction in 1634 of the packhouse, in which goods were weighed and stored and customs dues levied.

This period of considerable expansion was brought to an end with the Town Council's refusal in March 1638 to sign the National Covenant. This marked the beginning of Aberdeen's long involvement in the civil wars in Scotland. The burgh was occupied by armies, extra taxation had to be levied, some merchants were killed and others left the burgh. Foreign trade was little affected. But there was a tremendous decline in total trade. The receipts from the Shore Work duty fell from £555 in 1637-8 to £150 in 1639-40, a return to its level in 1600. Although some recovery took place in the early 1640s, total trade appears not to have exceeded its level in the 1610s. James Gordon, minister of Rothiemay wrote sadly in 1661

> Quhilst the civill warrs did overrun all, there wes no citie in Scot-
> land which did suffer more hurt than Aberdeen did, nor oftener,
> aither cessing, quartering, plundering, burning or slaughtering the
> inhabitants.

So much for trends in total trade. Which were the commercial growth points in the period? Firstly, trade with France
(Dieppe, Bordeaux and La Rochelle) increased except in the
early 1610s and (because of the war) in the late 1620s. The increase was linked to rising exports of salmon (for which France
was a major customer) and imports of salt (which came mainly
from La Rochelle, although also from Holland and Leith).
Secondly, trade in both directions with the Low Countries expanded — although passing through a lean period in the 1620s,
following which imports increased little. But exports increased
considerably throughout the period. There was an enormous expansion in the export of plaiding to the Low Countries — from
around 40,000 ells (an ell is thirty-seven inches) in the 1610s to
50,000 ells in 1630, 80,000 ells in 1636 and 120,000 ells in
1639. This growing volume of plaiding was a major factor in the
export boom of the 1630s. New manufactured commodities —
stockings, leather and gloves, indicating industrial diversification
in the burgh — played a part in increasing the volume of exports
to Flanders in the late 1620s. The third expanding sector of
trade was domestic sea-borne trade, especially with Leith. This
is more difficult to pinpoint than the other expanding trades —
because, since exports were not involved, the evidence of the exchequer records is not available. From the Shore Work Accounts,
however, it appears that the increase was partly in grain and
partly in miscellaneous goods brought into Aberdeen.

### Social mobility

Professor T.C. Smout attached importance, in his explanation
of the development of Glasgow, to the stimulus given by the
social structure of Glasgow. In particular, he praised the ease of
mobility in, and of entry into, the Glasgow merchant gild — and
contrasted the position in Aberdeen. So how did men enter the
merchant gild in Aberdeen and what scope was there for mobility
within the gild?6

The Burgess Register shows that most newly-admitted gild
burgesses had family ties with the gild (see Table 1). 65% of
those entering the gild between 1623 and 1626 were the sons of
gild burgesses. But there were three other important routes into
the gild. Few people took the first route — apprenticeship. The
second route — marriage to the daughter of a gild burgess —

1  apprenticeship          3  Payment of fee.
2  marriage

TABLE 1

*Reasons for Admission to Merchant Gild of all Burgesses admitted, 1623-1626*

| Reason for admission | Number admitted | % |
|---|---|---|
| Eldest sons of gild burgesses | 41 | 37.5 |
| Second sons of gild burgesses | 13 | 12 |
| Other sons of gild burgesses | 16 | 15 |
| Recommended by prominent men | 6 | 5.5 |
| Sons of craftsmen | 5 | 4.5 |
| Married daughter of gild burgesses | 8 | 7 |
| No connection stated | 20 | 18.5 |
| Total | 109 | 100 |

Source: *Miscellany of the New Spalding Club*, vols. i-ii
(1890, 1908)

provided a way in for 7% (who, the Stent Rolls show, were men of some substance before they won their ladies' hands). 5% of new gild burgesses were the sons of craftsmen (their fathers were among the wealthiest in the craft gild). But 19% could cite no connection with the gild. Accordingly, they paid a high entry fee (of 100 merks). It is not clear why most of these men joined the gild — they seem not to have traded overseas and were not particularly wealthy men. But the reasons for a few were crystal clear. For one group, the shipmasters, membership of the gild gave the right to trade on their own behalf (a clear source of extra income, since their voyages gave them a ready-made opportunity to trade). But despite this, the Stent Rolls do not suggest they got much wealthier as a result. A second group consisted of a few wealthy craftsmen — including one mason who had already appeared before the town council for usurping merchant privileges by trading in grain and malt. A third group were the cadets of landowners in the hinterland (though they mostly did not become active traders). And a few of the 19% prospered as a result of their membership of the gild. When Robert Ray was admitted in 1623 his stent was 38% of the burgh average. He became an active trader and by 1628 his stent was almost twice the burgh average. By 1637 his stent was four times the average and he was one of the twelve richest men in the burgh.

So routes existed into the gild, even for men without family connections. But they did not satisfy the demand for admission. There were always a few craftsmen usurping gild privileges by trading in foreign goods (like the goldsmith who bought deals of wood and tobacco) or reselling goods which they had not themselves manufactured. These craftsmen paid high stents by the standards of their fellow craftsmen and were prominent in the craft gilds. In a few cases, they were later admitted to the gild. But usually they were not. So there were always a few leading craftsmen eager to join the gild, but frustrated in their ambition. No doubt the burgh was the poorer for the lack of their energetic contribution to commerce.

Thus, though opportunities existed in Aberdeen for outsiders to join the gild, not everyone who wanted to was admitted. This was not a very different situation from Glasgow. There too, entry to the gild was determined mainly by family ties. It is true that a greater percentage of craftsmen joined the gild in Glasgow than in Aberdeen. But it is hard to say that this difference was crucial to the performance of the merchant gild.

Once a member of the gild, could the merchant become wealthy through commerce? It was certainly possible to specialise in commercial sectors which were prosperous and expanding. One of the richest men in the burgh, Robert Farquhar, specialised almost exclusively in the (expanding) local grain trade — and increased his stent from about twice the burgh average in 1616 to about four and a half times in 1628. Thomas Burnett, typical of merchants trading to Flanders in the 1620s and 1630s, was stented at only three-quarters of the burgh average when he was admitted to the gild in 1623. But by 1637 he was paying two and a quarter times the average stent. It seems, however, that merchants started their involvement in the profitable foreign trade to Flanders and France not by graduating through less profitable trade routes which involved less capital, but by launching straight in. Thomas Burnett started trading to Flanders the year he was admitted to the gild. The availability of borrowed capital, rather than the acquisition of experience and the slow build-up of wealth, seems to have been the passport to the most profitable foreign trading routes.

But, no matter how wealthy he became, it was not normally possible for the gild burgess to join the ruling elite of the burgh. This group, of about thirty-five or forty men, served frequently on the town council; were very wealthy; often owned land in the hinterland; were not always active traders; and were mostly the sons of gild burgesses (80% having entered the gild

Stent - an assessment, levy, tax.

Weigh-house or packhouse of Aberdeen, built in 1634. The building provided facilities for weighing and storing merchants' goods. Its construction reflects the growing trade of the burgh.

Coat of arms of the burgh of Aberdeen, as registered at the Lyon
Court in 1674.

by that means, compared with 65% of all new entrants). The election procedure in practice gave seats on the town council almost exclusively to members of a few leading families.

In short, though it was possible for craftsmen and unfree men to enter the merchant gild, not many were able to (and even for them it was not a passport to quick wealth). Others wished to join the gild but were prevented. Within the gild advancement was possible but the availability of the necessary capital seems to have been very important. And it was almost impossible to join the ruling elite.

### Did Aberdeen prosper?

We have seen that, until the outbreak of the civil war at least, Aberdeen's mercantile prosperity increased. The whole burgh also prospered. But Aberdeen's prosperity relative to many other burghs declined, as its share of the total burgh taxation (Table 2) shows. Why did Aberdeen not perform as well as the general run of burghs?

One factor may, as Professor Smout suggests, have been the relative lack of mobility into the merchant gild. But the difference in this respect between Aberdeen and Glasgow was slight. It is hard to imagine that this was a major factor.

TABLE 2

*Percentage of Total Scots Burgh Taxation levied on*
*Aberdeen, Glasgow, and Dundee*

|  | Aberdeen % | Glasgow % | Dundee % |
|---|---|---|---|
| 1601 | 8.00 | 4.50 | 10.75 |
| 1612 | 8.00 | 4.00 | 10.75 |
| 1635 | 8.00 | 5.50 | 9.33 |
| 1649 | 6.67 | 6.50 | 7.00 |
| 1670 | 7.00 | 12.00 | 6.10 |
| 1697 | 4.50 | 15.00 | 4.00 |

Sources: The burgh tax rolls are summarised in T.C. Smout, *Scottish Trade on the Eve of the Union, 1660-1707* (Edinburgh, 1963), 282-3, with the exception of that for 1635 which is in *Extracts from the Council Register of the Burgh of Aberdeen, 1625-42* (Scottish Burgh Record Society, 1871), 78-80.

The religious conservatism of Aberdeen has also been linked to its poor performance. It is true that Aberdeen responded only reluctantly to the challenge of the covenanting cause. It is true, too, that active covenanters were among the Aberdeen merchants who prospered: their religious radicalism may have fired their trading success. But many merchants who were not covenanters fared equally well or better.

More credibly, mercantile conservatism may have played a part. During the first half of the century there seems to have been only one Aberdeen burgess who traded to America; and Aberdeen merchants seem to have failed to exploit the growing demand for fish in Iberia. Nonetheless, they did adjust their trade routes and develop new commodities. A shortage of capital may be a further possible explanation. Certainly partnerships between Aberdeen burgesses seemed to have been uncommon, which must have hampered the funding of large (potentially profitable) ventures. But these theories are difficult to prove or disprove.

Flaws in the industrial structure of Aberdeen provide another possible explanation. Aberdeen's industry did expand and alter during the period (wool being manufactured into plaiding, and hides into leather, rather than being exported raw, for instance). But, although flax was available from the Baltic no linen industry grew up: and nor did the manufacture of new draperies.

The effect of the civil war was certainly a factor, Aberdeen being particularly badly affected and Glasgow relatively little. Geographical features may also have played a part. The hinterland of Aberdeen was perhaps less populous and less wealthy than that of Glasgow or Leith. But any difference seems too small to explain the different performance. More seriously, Aberdeen was simply on the wrong side of Scotland to be best-place for the main developing trade routes — to Ireland, America and the Mediterranean.

In short, social, industrial or commercial factors may have played a part in Aberdeen's relatively poor performance. But geography and war are likely to have been much more important — and it must not be forgotten that (as Table 2 shows) Aberdeen performed better than Dundee, Scotland's other major eastern port north of the Forth.

REFERENCES

1   The paper is based on part of the research undertaken in 1972-3 for
    an M. Litt thesis: D. Macniven *Merchant and Trader in Early Seven-
    teenth Century Aberdeen* (Aberdeen University M. Litt thesis, 1977).
    The thesis contains much additional information on many of the
    topics discussed here.

2   W. Kennedy *Annals of Aberdeen from the Reign of King William the
    Lion to the end of the year 1818* (2 vols., London, 1818) estimates
    (i, 186-7) the population at 7,805 in 1615. The parish registers
    (preserved in New Register House, Edinburgh) record 200 to 300
    births annually in the 1610s. At this period, the birth rate was nor-
    mally 30-40 per thousand population implying 6,000 to 12,000
    inhabitants, though the outer limits of that range are implausible.

3   The stent (tax) rolls in City of Aberdeen District Archives record
    about 350 gild burgesses: admissions to the gild are listed in A.M.
    Munro (ed.) 'Burgesses 1399-1631' and 'Aberdeen Burgess Register,
    1631-1700', *Miscellany of the New Spalding Club* vols. i and ii
    (1890, 1908).

4   This information comes mainly from the fascinating Shore Work
    Accounts (recording receipts from a tax levied on all trade through
    Aberdeen harbour): L.B. Taylor (ed.) *The Shore Work Accounts of
    Aberdeen 1596-1670* (Aberdeen, 1972).

5   Scottish Record Office, Exchequer Rolls (Custumers and Wine) E38
    series; Customs Accounts, E71/1/3.

6   There are three main sources of information about social mobility:
    (a) the Burgess Register (see note 3), which records the reason for
    the admission of each burgess to the gild,
    (b) the Stent Rolls, which contain individual tax assessments for
    most gild burgesses (eleven survive in the District Archives);
    (c) the Sasine Register (Scottish Record Office), which records trans-
    fers of land.

# 'MENACING THEIR PERSONS AND EXACTING ON THEIR PURSES'
# THE ABERDEEN JUSTICE COURT, 1657–1700

## GORDON DESBRISAY

### The justice court, its origins and nature

In cities and towns across the entire length and breadth of early modern Europe, civic magistrates shared, if little else, a fundamental concern with matters of public order and social control. They were often willing to go to great lengths on behalf of the privileged minorities they represented in order to impose their will, their mores, and their particular vision of urban society upon underprivileged, unrepresented majorities in Scotland. where a particularly virulent strain of civic authoritarianism prevailed, most burgh magistrates were busy, practical men with neither the time nor the inclination to analyse or theorise, on paper at least, about their various public duties, rules and obligations. One notable exception, however, was Aberdeen's Baillie Alexander Skene of Newtyle. Drawing on a lifetime's experience in and around civic government, in 1685 he published a remarkable book, *Memorials for the government of the royal burghs in Scotland*, a 'how-to' guide for burgh magistrates. On the vital question of how best to go about controlling the inherently unruly urban masses, he had this to say:

> It concerns all Magistrats very near, to be careful that no gross sin be indulged amongst them, such as Whoring, Drunkenness, and Swearing, these are the most common Scandalls unsuitable to the Gospel and such as profess it, that are to be found in Cities and Towns. These are sufficient to provoke God to withdraw his mercies, and to send sad Plagues and Rods, and confound all your Counsells and blast your best Endevours: for suppressing whereof, I know no better outward mean than a conscientious, faithfull, and diligent *Court of Justice* keeped by well principled Magisstrats assisted by pious, honest and zealous Constables weekly.[1]

Skene knew what he was talking about, for nearly thirty years before he had himself been one of the driving forces behind the establishment of just such a court.

The Aberdeen justice of the peace court, or 'justice court' as it was usually known, came into being in January 1657. Established ostensibly in response to a Cromwellian act of 1655 intended to revive the moribund commission of the peace in Scotland, in fact the Aberdeen justice court was the product of circumstances and developments rooted firmly within the town. The civic magistrates who presided over it took only what they wanted from the Cromwellian legislation, and showed no interest at all in the rest. In their hands, the justice court became a secular equivalent of the kirk session, whose particular brief ran 'especiallie to the punishing of uncleane persons, drunkards, cursers, and swearers, and breakers of the sabbath'.[2]

The very fact that Alexander Skene seemed to find it necessary to explain to Scotland's civic leaders exactly what a justice court was and what it had to offer, suggests that Aberdeen's example was unique. Indeed, judging from the few sets of justice court records known to survive from the period, it seems likely that Aberdeen's was the only urban justice court to remain active throughout the Restoration era, let alone to the end of the century and beyond.[3]

What was so special about Aberdeen? Why should it have needed, in effect, two kirk sessions when one might already seem to have been one too many? The answer was rooted in part in the dismal world of civic politics in the 1640s and 50s. A fundamental tenet of the covenanted kirk was that secular officials should remain divorced from, or better yet, subordinate to ecclesiastical authorities. Thus in Aberdeen the provost and baillies had, since the mid-1640s, been refused their customary seats on the kirk session. The result was that the magistrates and town council not only lost their once-powerful voice in the religious life of the community, but were also deprived of their right to participate in the all-important campaign to instil 'godly discipline' among the inhabitants.

Throughout the 1650s politics in the town centred on the town council's repeated efforts to reassert its authority over the burgh kirk. The minister and kirk session, not surprisingly, were just as determined to resist the council's advances. A series of direct and delightfully acrimonious confrontations ensued, the details of which need not concern us here.[4] Suffice it to say that in mid-seventeenth century Aberdonian politics, as in late twentieth century English football, every intricate attacking manoeuvre was countered by an unimaginative but numbingly effective defensive action.

The stalemate looked set to continue, and might have done so had it not been for the afore-mentioned Cromwellian act of

November 1655.[5] Twenty-seven of its thirty clauses were lifted
more or less intact from James VI's act of 1617, by which he
had made his final, unsuccessful bid to plant an English-style
justice of the peace in every parish. The Cromwellians, however,
made several crucial changes to the act. As it happens, they too
were finding it difficult to deal with the kirk, or, more pre-
cisely, the Scots ministry, whose members had by and large
proven resistant to even the most sugar-coated of their new
rulers' advances.[6] Thus it was that, in an attempt to loosen the
kirk's grip over the people, they gave justices of the peace the
right for the first time to enforce all acts of parliament concern-
ing public morals. It was these sections of the 1655 act, and
only these, which the Aberdeen magistrates latched on to.

Strange as it may seem, the establishment of the justice
court went some way towards healing the rift between civic and
church leaders in the town. It represented a compromise both
sides could live with. The magistrates could at last rejoin the
war on immorality and disorder, and church leaders could look
forward to secular cooperation in the one sphere in which it was
wanted, without having to concede any of their own sovereignty
over religious or ecclesiastical affairs. Nevertheless, it comes as
something of a surprise to find that the kirk session not only
acquiesced in the establishment of what was in essence a rival
institution, but actually cooperated with the officials of the
new court. The solution to this apparent riddle was to be found
outside the cloistered world of burgh politics. If Aberdeen's
secular and ecclesiastical leaders could agree on nothing else in the
1650s, they were united in their abhorrence of what they saw as
a rising tide of unruly, amoral, and licentious behaviour which
threatened to undermine the twin pillars of Christianity and
authoritarianism upon which their society rested. They were
deeply shocked to find 'howe hughlie God is provocked by the
frequent committing of the abhorable sin of fornicatioune in
this place, quhich is come to so great a height throw the louse-
ness of the tyme, that it cannot but presage some great judgement in this citie'.[7]

There was no great mystery as to the immediate cause of
this apparent surge in illicit sexual activity. The answer lay in
the fact that throughout the 1650s Aberdeen played host to an
unprecedented number of young, unmarried men and women.
In winter, when the English garrison was normally at full strength,
roughly 1,000 soldiers — one to every seven inhabitants — were
billeted in the town. Their presence as much as doubled the
adult male population of the burgh. Nor were they the only

large group of newcomers to descend upon the town. Hundreds of young Scots, men and women, flocked to Aberdeen in these same years, quite independent of the army. They came to find work. In the last, savage outbreak of plague in 1647-8, over 1,700 townsfolk had perished: a high proportion of the adult dead had been servants, journeymen, and petty craftsmen, many of whom had originally come from outside the burgh. Now their replacements, who normally would have arrived in a steady trickle over the course of many years, swarmed in to take up the sudden vacancies.[8]

The inevitable temptations which such a confluence of young people was bound to excite were no doubt amplified and compounded by conditions in the town. Soldiers and servants alike were forced to live in overcrowded and unsettled conditions. While many of the English troops based in Aberdeen strove to live lives of exemplary piety and purity, others seized the opportunity to indulge in traditional soldierly recreations. With the spectre of renewed warfare never far off, an undercurrent of violence and eroticism pervaded the town: dozens of local girls were delated for having 'fallen in fornication' with a soldier, and during the occupation the birth-rate remained more than twenty-percent above the level of the previous decade.[9] The local economy, although it revived somewhat after 1653, remained less than buoyant. Many of those who came to Aberdeen expecting to find work found none, and more than a few turned to vagrancy, crime, and prostitution. In the difficult economic climate couples who might have preferred to legitimise their sexual relationships much earlier were forced to postpone marrying: church officials noted in August 1654 'the increase of the sin of fornicatioune, not onlie be single persones, but also be sundrie other persones under pretence of marriage'.[10]

Alexander Skene happened to be a baillie in 1657, and thus he automatically became one of the original justices of the peace in Aberdeen, along with the three other baillies and the provost. He had also been a leading member of the kirk session, and was well acqainted with the upsurge in promiscuity and, indeed, 'all sorts of Sin and Impietie' in the burgh. He proved an energetic and effective justice of the peace, and was responsible for launching a campaign to extract fines on the spot from those heard to curse or swear in public. He was later to boast that within six months, 'one would not have heard the meanest oath in the streets on a mercat day, though there would have been several thousands of Countrey and Town's people on the streets'.[11]

His more lasting achievement, however, lay in helping to de-
fine a distinctive role for the justice of the peace court within
the overall framework of authority and discipline in the burgh.
As an active and loyal member of the kirk session, he presumably had no desire to see that organization's long-standing campaign to enforce godly discipline — so central to the kirk of
Scotland's divinely-ordained mission — completely eclipsed by
the new court. Nor it seems, did very many others. What Skene
and most of his colleagues within the civic establishment clearly
did feel, however, was that the censures imposed by the church
were no longer sufficient to deter young people from straying
from the straight and narrow. Acts of parliament enabling magistrates to inflict financial and bodily mortifications on drunkards, blasphemers, and fornicators, among others, had long been
in place but had seldom been invoked in the burgh because it
had generally been felt that matters of indiscipline and immorality could safely be left to the kirk. In the face of the unruly and
licentious behaviour which so alarmed civic and church leaders
alike in the 1650s, however, it was perhaps inevitable that the
idea of meting out harsher penalties would gain new currency.

Alexander Skene was one of those who understood from
the outset that it was with regard to punishments that the Aberdeen justice court could make a unique and lasting contribution
to the forces of social control in the burgh. The justice court and
the kirk session can be shown to have differed hardly at all in
the ways in which they went about identifying, apprehending,
trying, and convicting moral delinquents, but the two courts
diverged sharply when it came to punishing offenders. A couple
convicted of fornication, for example, could normally expect to
be dealt with by both courts. Upon delation (accusation), the
session would place them under church censure, barring them
from receiving the sacraments; following the inevitable con-
viction, both parties would be required to undergo a ritual public humiliation which involved three consecutive Sunday appear-
ances before the congregation, barefoot, dressed in sackcloth,
and seated upon the 'stool of repentance'; having completed
their penance, they could then expect to be absolved of their
sin and welcomed back into the bosom of the church. The justice court's punishments were rather more prosaic. Fornication
normally elicited a fine of £10, payable immediately upon con-
viction. Those who could easily afford to pay £10, paid more:
those who could not pay faced one or more of an array of corporal punishments at the magistrate's disposal. These could
involve encounters with the lash, the 'jougs' (a heavy iron collar

chained to a wall), or the stocks, incarceration in the Tolbooth prison, and forceful expulsion or banishment from the town.

The justice court, then, provided Aberdeen's civic elite with a systematic means of reinforcing the kirk's long, drawn out cycle of condemnation, retribution, and reconciliation with a 'short, sharp, shock' of its own. By adding the likelihood of financial or physical distress to the threat of condemnation and humiliation, the city fathers hoped to deter potential miscreants and so turn back the tide of ungodly behaviour which they feared would yet engulf them all. Would it not, however, have been possible — particularly after the Restoration, when magistrates in Aberdeen and elsewhere returned to the kirk session — for the ecclesiatical authorities to administer these additional punishments themselves? This, after all, seems to have been what happened in other burghs, where the upstart justice courts were allowed to wind down after 1660. There was an influential body of opinion in Aberdeen, however, which insisted that separate courts really were necessary. Alexander Skene was one of a number of prominent civic figures whose views on the matter of church-state relations had recently been re-shaped under the influence of English Independency, a religious movement which, like Quakerism in succeeding decades, made considerable inroads among the ruling establishment in Aberdeen, and virtually nowhere else in Scotland, in the 1650s.[12] For Skene, the issue was quite straightforward. 'In this Polemick-Age', he wrote in his *Memorials* of 1685, 'when many things are controverted, which were not questioned formerly, it is found a matter very extrinsick to Church-Officers or Guides, to meddle with any thing that is propper to the Civil-Magistrat, such as Fynes, Imprisonments, or Corporall Punishments'.[13] Thus, as far as he was concerned the temporal authority of the church was subject to strict limitations. It was a point he felt called upon to repeat, this time even more emphatically:

> It may be easie to any understanding men to perceive how heterodit a thing it is to see Preachers speaking to such delinquents more Magisterially, liker a Civil Magistrat than Ministerially, menacing their Persons and exacting on their Purses, whereas it were more becoming Ministers of the Gospell to endevour to awaken and convince their Consciences, which is their propper work, because the Weapons of their Warfare should not be Carnall. (2 Cor. 10-14)[14]

Skene was not arguing that the kirk should cease to be involved in the business of godly discipline — only that it was

limited in the actions it could rightfully take against those stray
members of its flock convicted of misdeeds. The religious im-
pulses behind this viewpoint, which had helped to provide the
Aberdeen justice court with the advantage of firm ideological
and theological underpinnings in its early days, were discredited
soon after the Restoration, and those who espoused them de-
barred from public office. By then, however, the new court had
more than proven its worth. Burgh magistrates of all shades of
opinion valued the maintenance of public order above virtually
all else in civic life, and having given the new court a fair chance,
they could see that a kirk session and a justice court, acting
separately but in close cooperation, complementing and compounding each other's authority, offered burgh magistrates a
total capacity for social control which exceeded the sum con-
tributions of its parts. As Skene himself put it,

> Neither is this design to weaken their hands, but to strengthen
> them in their propper work; seeing the end of both Courts is to
> suppress Sin, and it is the more likely to take the desired effect,
> when Civil and Ecclesiastick Rulers do every one their Duty in
> their proper Sphere.[15]

## Justice court personnel

During their one-year term of office, the civic magistrates who
doubled as justices of the peace in Aberdeen enjoyed varying
but always significant degrees of influence over virtually every
governmental, judicial, educational, and religious institution
in the burgh. Their job as justices of the peace was to sit in
judgement, each Monday morning at 9 a.m., on all those brought
before them. Being the busy men that they were, however, they
can have had little time to spare for the justice court: virtually
all of the work outside of court hours, therefore, had to be
done by others.

The real backbone of the justice court was the constabulary,
a corps of middle and lower-middle class townsmen willing to
inspect, and if necessary intervene in the private lives of their
fellow inhabitants. Each October roughly thirty to thirty-five
constables were appointed by the magistrates to twelve month
terms of office, and over the forty-three years under review it
has proved possible to identify 466 separate men as having
served an average of three terms each.[16]

What were they expected to do? Their disciplinary duties
and methods were almost indistinguishable from those of the
thirty-five to forty kirk session personnel, with whose juris-
diction they overlapped. They were distributed evenly over the

town, with each man assigned to a particular precinct. Each year the constables were given a long list of responsibilities, but it is clear that their main job was to pry into the personal lives of their constituents.[17] Exactly how they were to acquire the dirt on their neighbours is not made altogether clear in the records. Whether they patrolled their precincts like bobbies on a beat, listened at doors and peered through windows and key-holes, or simply relied on gossip, hearsay, and common know-ledge, we shall probably never know.

Just who were these men who were apparently so willing to stoke the engines of Aberdeen's great machinery of social con-trol? The occupations of roughly two-thirds of all constables can be discerned from the records. Predictably, they were mainly recruited from the upper third of Aberdeen's socio-economic ladder. In common with the deaconry of the kirk session, on which more than half of the constables served at one point or another, about two-thirds of them were craftsmen, and one quarter merchants. These merchant constables tended to be petty retailers, and ought not to be confused with the pros-perous merchants with overseas connections such as dominated local affairs. Indeed, no merchant constable was ever elected to the town council, and only a few ever rose to be elders in the kirk. Constables, then, can safely, if rather awkwardly, be said to have been drawn from the bottom half of the upper third of urban society. Theirs was the least prestigious of the town's many public offices, and the one least likely to lead to advance-ment.

One of the most startling facts to emerge from a study of the justice court personnel is, however, that a good number of the constables, somewhere in the order of 25-30%, were selected from amongst the town's swollen ranks of non-burgesses, the 'unfree' men who belonged to neither craft nor guild. This fact seems at first sight to cast some doubt on the accepted view of urban society in early modern Scotland, which holds that 'To the burgesses alone belonged the privileges of being members of a burgh: the rest of the inhabitants were mere indwellers', with no more right to participate in civic administration 'than a country bumpkin from the landward pairts'.[18]

Upon closer examination, however, the admission of non-burgesses to the constabulary becomes the exception which proves the rule. The unfreemen appointed represented not so much the vanguard of incipient urban democracy, as the rear-guard of the established ruling oligarchy. Almost without ex-ception, the unfree constables were chosen from just one rung

below the burgess classes — they too can be said to have belonged
to the fortunate upper third of civic society. Most were born in
Aberdeen, and a fair proportion had served at least part of an
apprenticeship. Skilled and semi-skilled workers, trusted servants and employees of wealthy merchants and well-to-do craftsmen, it was possible for them to enjoy a standard of living comparable to that of many burgesses, and which the majority of
the populace could only envy. The decision to admit such men
to the constabulary was not based on any desire on the part of
the magistrates to expand the franchise or otherwise alter the
established structure of society: it was simply a matter of logist-
ics and expediency. The business of social control as practiced
in early modern Scotland was an extremely labour-intensive
one, nowhere more so than in Aberdeen. Even before 1657,
when the burgh's disciplinary machinery centred on the town
council and kirk session, as many as fifty burgesses a year were
needed to run the apparatus. With the advent of the justice of
the peace court, the number jumped to more than eighty. This
presented city leaders with something of a dilemma. During the
first decade of the court's existence the total number of merchant and craft burgesses active at any one time can be said
with some accuracy to have been about 400 out of a total population of roughly 7,500.[19] In the past it had proved possible to
place as many as one in every eight burgesses in public office
each year, but the prospect of recruiting one man in five
seemed more than the burgess community could comfortably
bear.

So far as is known, no other town in Scotland, and few if
any in early modern England or Europe, could count on its
citizens for such an astounding degree of participation in the
day-to-day maintenance of law and order. Of the nearly 500
men appointed to the constabulary over the years studied, only
one refused to serve, and he was already on the kirk session. Although we may never fully understand all of the reasons for this
remarkable consensus, it was clearly this bedrock of support
upon which the entire structure of authority and discipline in
Aberdeen rested.

### Trends in justice court activities

The types of cases pursued by the Aberdeen justice of the peace
court between 1657 and 1700 can be divided into four main
categories. The first, sexual offences, usually accounted for the
majority of the entries in the court register. The 'uncleane persons' referred to above were all those who engaged in pre- or

extra-marital sexual relations. Adultery, in which one or both parties were married, was the most serious single offence dealt with by the court, while fornication, involving unmarried couples, was by far the most common. Those who 'fell in fornication' a second time were known as 'relapses', and on occasion 'trelapses' and even 'quadralapses' were uncoverd and prosecuted. Ante-nuptial fornication, involving couples planning to wed, was a slightly lesser offence, as was 'scandalous carriage', a somewhat nebulous term applied to various sorts of impropriety short of sexual intercourse, or, more commonly, to those people suspected of fornication or adultery but against whom no conclusive evidence could be brought.[20]

Disorderly conduct, the second category, encompassed drunkenness, cursing and swearing, disturbing the peace, scolding, striking or injuring another, abusing or refusing to assist a constable of the court, or any combination of the above. When committed on a Sunday these acts often, but not always, elicited a heavier penalty. Other, more clear-cut cases of Sabbath breach included not only failure to attend church for reasons other than infirmity or ill health, but a whole range of activities perfectably acceptable during the week but proscribed on the day of rest, such as selling or consuming drink in time of sermon, walking in the fields, working, or, most commonly, fishing.[21]

The fourth category, undesirable persons, included cases which, unlike most of those listed above, had seldom been of particular concern to the kirk session. They involved the justice court not so much in the repression of behaviour deemed antisocial or irreligious, as in the removal from the town of potentially disruptive elements. These included vagrants and other outsiders who arrived with 'no way of living' or no 'testificate' of good character from the minister of their previous parish; 'unfamous persons' such as those who returned to the town after having been banished; residents who received the 'unfamous' into their homes; and those convicted of theft.

Using these four headings, subdivided into the most common types of cases, a detailed court profile can be constructed for each of the justice court's first thirty years of operation, when a readily quantifiable register of convictions was kept. It is then possible to plot the annual figures on a graph so as to get a picture of trends in court activity over time. Two things are immediately apparent from the line in Figure 1 representing the total number of cases dealt with each year. The first is that court activity varied widely from year to year: in 1665, for example, eighty-five cases were handled, as compared with sixty

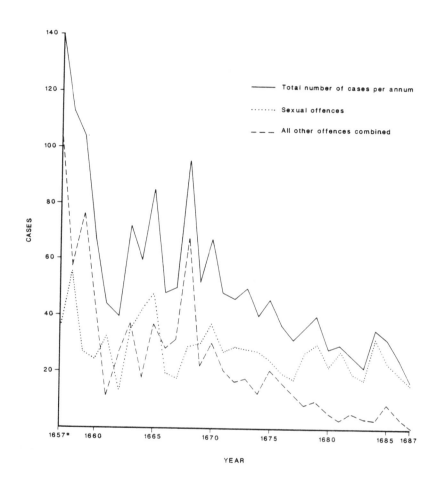

Figure 1   Trends in justice court activity,
Aberdeen, 1657-1687

Note:   the official council year, and therefore the year adopted
by the justic court, commenced just prior to Michaelmas (29
September). The court's initial 'year' lasted only nine months
(January—September, 1657), making the figures for that 'year'
all the more remarkable.

the year before and forty-eight the year after. Equally obvious is the fact that these annual, short-term fluctuations were transcended over the long term by a fairly steady trend towards a diminution of the annual caseload, from a peak of 140 cases in 1657, to a low of just seventeen in 1687.

A third important trend can be seen when the total caseload is broken down into case types. For the sake of simplicity only two categories are shown on Figure 1, sexual offences and all others combined. These lines clearly chart the process by which the activities of the Aberdeen justice court came to be almost completely dominated by crimes of the flesh. By 1670, sexual offences took up more than 50% of the court's business each year, a proportion which by the 1680s seldom dipped below 80%, and, based on the available evidence, may well have topped 90% in the closing decade of the century. It was not that ever-increasing numbers of sexual misdeeds were being uncovered, however, it was simply that over the years there were fewer and fewer prosecutions of disorderly conduct, Sabbath breach, and undesirable persons. Thus, although the number of sexual offences prosecuted between 1657 and 1686 actually fell by an average of 8% every five years, this was less than one-half the rate at which the total caseload diminished, and — most importantly — less than one-quarter the rate at which prosecutions for all other types of offences combined fell.

What are we to make of these trends? Interesting as they may be on their own, we can only really hope to make sense of them when they are examined in conjunction with a wide range of other matters relating to the town in these years. To begin with, it is important to distinguish between the short and long-term factors at work. It is the short-term factors which account for the jagged peaks and troughs that distort the otherwise quite steady downward slope of long-term developments in court activity. Although it is next to impossible to identify and assess each and every agent and circumstance impinging upon the court in a given year, a number of the more common variables can be noted. The forces of nature, for example, could clearly influence the court's work: in 1697, when, as Dr Tyson has shown, poor weather and serious food shortages led to disease and high mortality, the justice court sat only thirteen times. Although difficult to prove, it seems likely that backlogs of cases occasionally built up, to be dealt with in subsequent years by more active or less beleaguered members of the justice court. It is also important to remember that a degree of discontinuity was virtually assured by the huge (about 60%) annual turnover in personnel. We have already seen how one energetic baillie could affect the work of the court, and a handful of especially vigilant (or lax) constables could presumably impose their stamp on the proceedings as well.

Even when the particular circumstances involved in a specific surge, or lapse, or shift in court activity can be identified, however, they cannot adequately explain the more important, lasting changes which occurred between 1657 and 1700. The long-term factors which alone can account for the decreasing case-load of the justice court and the increasing preoccupation with sexual offences associated with it can be divided into three overlapping categories. The first concerns changes within the court itself, or rather within the men who made up the court. From its establishment in 1657 to the end of the century, no adjustments were made to the basic organisational and proceedural structure of the justice court. Neither did the basic types of men, in terms of occupational, financial, and social background, elected to the magistracy or appointed to the constabulary vary appreciably over the years. The important changes, then, appear to have been ones of attitude and inclination.

Such developments, of course, are difficult to pinpoint and impossible to quantify. Nevertheless, it seems quite clear that the determination and reforming zeal which motivated Aberdeen's early justices of the peace and which contributed to the tremendously high rates of court activity, was far less prevalent, if not altogether absent, in many of their successors. Skene felt called upon to remind a new generation of magistrates in 1685 that managing the justice court was akin to a religious duty, which 'tho never so much strengthened and established by Law, may through remissness and want of true Zeal be also turned into a meer form, without any fruit or affect'.[22] His day, however, had long since passed. The covenanting generation eventually gave way after the Restoration to a new breed of men, rather less censorious, somewhat more tolerant, and altogether less inclined to burden themselves with the immense task of rooting out each and every example of wayward behaviour. It was this last trait which may help to explain the court's mounting tendency to concentrate on crimes of the flesh. With a pregnancy almost always involved in such cases as came to light, they were the easiest for the authorities to detect, and the most difficult for the accused to deny.

Nevertheless, it would be quite wrong to ascribe the steady decline in the number of prosecutions for non-sexual offences wholly to a growing sense of magnanimity tinged with sloth on

the part of the magistrates and their minions. This would be to
assume a constant level of misdemeanour over a period of more
than forty years, and such was patently not the case. The justice
court, after all, owed its very existence in part to a well docu-
mented upsurge in rowdy and licentious behaviour. The records
of the court's first frantic years reinforce the impression that
the panic-stricken declarations of civic and church leaders alike
in the mid-1650s owed more to realistic appraisals of the actual
situation in the town than to any over-heated puritanical imagin-
ings. And as the conditions that spawned the unrest slowly
ceased, this too was reflected in the gradual slackening off of
court activity.

Of the many factors which combined to disrupt and destab-
ilise Aberdonian society in the 1650s, the most important of all,
as discussed above, was the over-abundance of adolescents and
young adults in the town, many of whom were but recently
arrived and remained unsettled in their new surroundings. This
demographic and social imbalance, however, gradually righted
itself, and as it did so much of the hedonistic boisterousness of
the Cromwellian period subsided. A turning point was the departure of the English garrison late in 1659, and with it a
smaller army of wives, children, servants, and girlfriends, followed
in subsequent months by an additional score of young women
with no visible means of support who were rounded up and expelled by the justice court in the course of a 'mopping-up'
exercise.

The sudden exodus of several hundred people, mostly
young and single, and including among them many of the most
disruptive elements in the town, had an immediate and lasting
impact upon the community. Over the next three to five years
the number of live births recorded fell by nearly twenty percent,
prosecutions for fornication and adultery declined by forty percent, and cases of Sabbath breach and disorderly conduct plum-
meted by seventy and eighty percent respectively. Neither the
birth rate nor the various crime rates remained so depressed for
very long, but to the end of the century none of these indices
— especially those concerned with non-sexual forms of indiscipline — ever again registered a sustained pitch of activity to
quite match that of the exuberant 1650s.

Apart from effecting a massive and almost instaneous shift
in the demographic balance of the town, the departure of the
troops and their consorts also signalled the beginning of a less
spectacular, long-term change in the make-up of the population.
By the time the garrison pulled out in 1659, the flood of young

Scots who had poured into Aberdeen from throughout the
North East for the better part of a decade had slowed to a
trickle. By 1670 it had all but dried up. The reasons for this
seem clear enough. Aberdeen did not recover fully from the
'troublous' years of the 1640s and 1650s, either in terms of
population or prosperity. Opportunities which may once have
seemed so bright failed to materialise for many of the newcomers. After the Restoration, economic growth remained at
best slow but steady. A move to Aberdeen was no longer as
attractive a proposition as it had once been. A sharp fall in
immigration, combined with a birth rate which changed relatively little between 1660 and 1700, was to further reduce Aberdeen's once hugely disproportionate number of rumbustious
and potentially troublesome young people.[23]

It was not just that from 1659 on there appear to have been
successively fewer youths around to make trouble, however. It
must also be considered that the generations which grew to
maturity after 1657 did so in a rather different environment.
Most of them grew up in less crowded conditions, for example,
and few were exposed to the unedifying role-models presented
by soldiers at leisure. Perhaps more importantly, a higher proportion were born and raised in the town, and so were subjected
at a very early age to Aberdeen's expanded system of social control. And to a certain extent the system appears to have worked.

A third factor, then, which cannot be ignored in seeking to
explain the long-term trends in justice court activity was the
cumulative effect of year after year of relentless repression
aimed at imposing and maintaining both earthly and godly discipline in the burgh. The run-away indiscipline and immorality
of the 1650s had been met by an unprecedented campaign to
bring the full force of civic government and authority to bear
upon the problem. The creation of the justice court effectively
doubled the town's total capacity for social control, adding
thirty or so constables to the thirty-six elders and deacons of
the kirk session, and, perhaps more importantly, compounding
the punishments meted out to transgressors. Faced with a far
higher likelihood of being apprehended, convicted, and saddled
with a burdensome penalty, many an unruly Aberdonian must
have begun to have had second thoughts about wandering from
the straight and narrow. The sharp decline in the number of
prosecutions for non-sexual offences, in particular, almost certainly reflected a real fall in the incidence of such activity, and
can therefore be regarded as something of a victory for the
forces of law and order in the town.

The victory, however, was a somewhat limited one. As we have seen, prosecutions for fornication and adultery, the forms of indiscipline most disruptive to the community and abhorrent to its leaders, declined only very slightly and gradually over the period. The percentage of live births conceived out of wedlock appears only to have declined over the period 1657-1687 from 16% to just under 11%. What decline there was in illicit sexual activity was probably due as much to the fall in the number of young people in the town as to anything else. Why, then, was sexual misconduct so much less susceptible than other forms of indiscipline to the types of pressure that the justice court and its allied judiciaries could bring to bear? One obvious point was that in most healthy people the sex drive was rather stronger and more deeply rooted, than, say, the urge to curse, swear, or skip church. However strong the underlying instinct, though, the fact remained that illicit sexual relations nearly always involved the positive, conscious consent of both partners, and despite the best efforts of the town's ruling classes, over the years that consent continued to be forthcoming.[24]

### Offenders and their fates

As discussed earlier, it was with regard to matters of punishment that the Aberdeen justice court established a distinctive role and identity for itself within the overall framework of authority and social control in the burgh. The kirk session, once it decided to pursue an individual, showed relatively little concern for the economic and social distinctions of this world. All men, at least when doing penance, were more or less equal in the eyes of the Lord and His kirk — as the wearing of sackcloth was intended to signify. The justice court, however, took a quite different approach to the common task of bringing those who had strayed back to the path of Christian and civic righteousness. If the kirk session can be said to have worked on men and women from the inside out, the justice court worked from the outside in: to paraphrase Alexander Skene (see above, p. 75) the Weapons of their Warfare were decidedly Carnall, being based almost entirely upon the imposition of financial and bodily mortifications.

It was necessary, then, for the civic magistrates who presided over the justice court to pay close attention to the differences between the various categories and classes of offenders brought before them, and to scale their sentences accordingly. In common with judicial authorities throughout Scotland and across much of early modern Europe, the Aberdeen magistrates tended to tailor their punishments as much to the criminal as to the crime.[25] Although there were standard punishments established by law for each type of offence, in practice sentencing was carried out at the magistrates' discretion. This enabled them to take into account not only the nature and severity of the offence but also such factors as the age, sex, marital status, past history, occupation, wealth, and social standing of the parties involved. In a society of such extremes of wealth and poverty, privilege and powerlessness, it could hardly have been otherwise. The men who ruled the town were, after all, driven not by devotion to any notion of blind jusitce, but by a clear-eyed, wholly pragmatic appreciation of what would, in their view, best serve the interests of their community.

A full discussion of the justice court's varied and often draconian system of punishments, pecuniary and corporal, is not possible in this paper.[26] One or two examples, however, can be used to illustrate the inherent inequalities of civic society which were both reflected and reinforced by the justice court. When the well-to-do were convicted (invariably for sexual offences) they could expect to pay a fine, with especially wealthy men being ordered to pay well above the standard rate. In 1680, for example, John Sandilands, a prosperous and well-connected merchant in his mid-twenties, was fined £40, four times the usual rate, for his fall in fornication with a servant by the name of Jean Burnet.[27] His good name, it seems, was only temporarily besmirched, however, for ten years later he was elected provost and thus empowered to sit in judgement over other fornicators. Had Sandilands not been so rich, he would have been asked to pay the normal £10. Men like Sandilands could rest assured that they would never have to face the sorts of horrific corporal punishments visited all too often on sexual and other offenders from the lower orders. Money might not have bought happiness in seventeenth century Aberdeen, but it could certainly buy exemption from some of life's more gruesome ordeals.

Those who suffered most at the hands of the justices of the peace were the young, the poor, and the female, and those who fell into all three categories were often made to bear the full brunt of the magistrates' fury. In theory men and women were to be treated in exactly the same way by the court. The 1655 and 1661 acts which re-established justices of the peace in Scotland were careful to note that all pecuniary penalties 'shall be levied, not only of the Man, but also of the Woman, according to her quality, and degree of her Offence'.[28] If the law was equitable, though, society was not. The overwhelming majority of women convicted, particularly for sexual offences, were young servants. If the £10 fine for fornication represented three weeks work for a semi-skilled journeyman, and five weeks work for a male labourer, it was an entire year's wages for even the most senior female servant in a household. The second rank servants earned just £8 spending money a year. Even when a relative or employer was willing to cover a girl's penalty, it would have taken years of arduous labour and careful saving to repay them. And it must be remembered that since most sexual offences came to light after the girl became pregnant, she also had to contend with the dangers, expenses and responsibilities involved in bearing and raising a child.

Nowhere were the iniquities of seventeenth century burgh life more graphically displayed than in the Aberdeen justice court's handling of cases of adultery. It was the offence which drew the harshest of the court's punishments. Not only was it a contravention of the seventh commandment, it was also regarded as an assault on three of western society's most fundamental institutions: marriage, the family, and the inheritance of property. It was almost certainly seen also as an affront to the cherished heirarchical structure of society. Adulterous couples usually represented the civic community at its most polarized, for almost invariably the affair involved an older, married man from the privileged middle and upper classes, and a young, single girl from the wholly 'unfree' lower classes. More often than not it was an 'upstairs-downstairs' relationship, between the master of a household and one of his servants.

The standard fine for adultery was £40. Three-quarters of the fifty or so men convicted between 1657 and 1700 managed to pay the fines, as compared to just one-quarter of the women. Those of both sexes who could not pay were compelled to submit to a variety of corporal punishments and public humiliations. In 1667 John Reid, a married tailor, was convicted of having had an affair with Elpet Johnstone, a servant.[29] It was apparent to the magistrates that neither of them could hope to raise enough money to pay the fines: they were both, therefore, sentenced to be whipped, with thirty 'stripes' each, and then conveyed by the hangman to the limits of the Freedom Lands and banished from the town. Banishment was perhaps the most devastating punishment meted out by the justice court, and was reserved for notorious thieves, the occasional prostitute, penurious adulterers, and most convicted adulteresses.

A typical case of adultery recorded in 1678 contains a vivid account of what banishment normally involved. Agnes Brinder,

a servant, was convicted of having fallen in 'pregnant and mani-
fest scandall of adultrie' with her master, William Murray, a
weaver and a married man. He was ordered to pay £40, and was
imprisoned 'during the magistrates pleasure'. If, as the court's
financial accounts suggest, he paid his fine promptly, he is un-
likely to have remained in the Tolbooth for very long. Agnes,
however, was not given the opportunity to pay a fine. She was
to be held in prison until Friday, the day of the market. She
was then to be publicly and forcibly banished from the town. In
the words of the magistrates, she was to be put on

> ane kairt and cartit efter ane hors, with ane croune of paper on
> her head declairing her guiltines, and to be takin doune the streit
> to the Greine and there whipit befir the said William his house,
> and therafter conveyit be the hangman along to the bow bridge
> and banished.[30]

A more degrading spectacle would be difficult to imagine. Cast
out of the community, cut off from family and friends in the
town, or if born elsewhere, forced to try to return home in dis-
grace — it was a secular form of excommunication. (Indeed, the
church invariably brought sentence of excommunication
into effect against those found guilty of adultery.) Without
a testificate of good behaviour from the town's minister, Agnes
Brinder and others like her could well find it difficult to
settle in any other parish in the region: to judge from the attitudes of the Aberdeen authorities, young unmarried and un-
employed women were seldom welcome additions to any town,
even if they did not have a criminal record. Unwelcome virtually everywhere they went, the sentence of banishment may
well have condemned some of these women to a life of vagrancy, and quite possibly even an early death. To return to
Aberdeen unbidden would be to invite a repetition of their
ordeal, augmented by being branded on the face or hand with
the iron used to burn the town's coat of arms onto barrels of
salmon, or 'doukit' in the sea, strapped into a special seat (designed by Alexander Skene) affixed to the crane at the quay-
side. In the chilling words of one magistrate, the banished who
dared return without permission could expect to be 'roughly
punishit, according to *justice*'.[31] Rough justice, indeed.